SOLUTION TO MASS UNEMPLOYMENT IN NIGERIA

Prompting Accelerated Industrialisation Through Linking
Education and Production

No. 1 in the series, *Achieving Rapid Industrialisation and Democratisation in Nigeria*

By

F. E. OGBIMI

Technology Planning and Development Unit (TPDU)
Obafemi Awolowo University
Ile-Ife, Nigeria.

SOCIETY FOR LINKING EDUCATION AND
PROBLEMS PUBLICATION, OBAFEMI AWOLOWO
UNIVERSITY, ILE-IFE, NIGERIA.

SOLUTION TO MASS UNEMPLOYMENT IN NIGERIA

Prompting Accelerated Industrialisation through Linking Education and Production

No. 1 in the series, *Achieving Rapid Industrialization and Democratization in Nigeria*

ISBN 978-041-109-7

Third Printing, June, 2007

Second Printing, 2003

First Printing, 1999

©Professor Francis Eniterai Ogbimi

Typesetted by: **Tayo Ogunleke**

Printed by Obafemi Awolowo University Press Limited, Ile-Ife, Nigeria.

DEDICATION

This series is dedicated to my brother, the late Mr. S.K. Ogbimi.

PREFACE

The series, *Achieving Rapid Industrialisation and Democratisation in Nigeria*, is a product of accident and curiosity. It is also a product symbolic of a break with an intellectual tradition.

The social scientists have long dominated the influential area of development theory and planning. Therefore, no one expects one who had acquired a Bachelor's degree in Agricultural Science, Master's and Doctoral degrees in Polymer Science (science of rubbers and plastics) – a scientist, to pursue a career as a development theorist and planner.

However, through the accident of sojourning, I became curious as from the early 1980s to understand the basis of the present global distribution of wealth and how wealth is created. The research to satisfy my wild dream started in 1986. My research efforts have been blessed abundantly. It is my firm belief that the generous reward for my efforts are gifts to mankind; they are not for any individual or nation.

There is a lot of fear and hopelessness in the world today. Ignorance is the main cause of fear and hopelessness. This series will certainly increase man's understanding of key global problems like unemployment, low productivity, lack of industrialisation and poverty, and reduce fear and hopelessness. The series is therefore for everyone to read. Everyone on earth should read all the titles in the series so that all the peoples in the world should soon be able to say with one voice, *'we shall control our destinies; we shall not allow our destinies to control us anymore.'*

You owe mankind and indeed yourself the responsibility of understanding the problems in the world you live in. This is how you can contribute to finding solutions to them. Discuss the solutions proferred in this book with other persons.

ACKNOWLEDGEMENT

The assistance of many individuals and groups made the research that produced this series possible. I am grateful to all the people who typed the manuscripts, especially Mrs. F. Ogunweide, Mrs. O. Akanji, Mrs. R.O. Abah, Mrs. E. Olanrewaju and Mr. E.O. Ajayi. I am also grateful to Messrs R.B. Ajala and K. Lauck who helped in preparing some of the illustrations in the series.

Those who read my research papers in the peer review process and agreed or disagreed with my positions played a unique role. I appreciate their assistance. I also appreciate the roles of my colleagues and students, especially those in the Faculty of Technology, Obafemi Awolowo University, Ile-Ife, Nigeria. The various questions raised and views expressed by my peers, colleagues and students over the years helped to expand the scope of my analyses. I am grateful to Professor J. I. Ighalo, Faculty of Environmental Design and Management, Obafemi Awolowo University, Ile-Ife, Nigeria, for encouraging me to prepare this series.

I am particularly grateful to Mr. and Mrs. J.O. Erusiafe, for their material and moral support. I also appreciate the support of the Avwunu family, especially, the assistance of Joseph, George, Nelson, Edith and Sunday. The support of Professor and Mrs. M.B. Salami, Professor and Mrs. E.A. Aduayi, Professor and Mrs. P. E. Oribabor, the late Mr. B.M. Salami and Mrs. M. O. Salami, Dr. & Mrs. M. Omosule, Dr. (Mrs.) S. Williams, Mrs. D. I. Ocan, Mrs. E. M. Jeje and the late Mrs. J. N. Dixon, I appreciate. Rev. Fathers C. Iheme, A. Amoako-Attah and Dr. D. Oyesola, O. P., were particularly valuable. I also appreciate their assistance.

I am especially grateful to my larger family for the traditions of honesty, hardwork, perseverance and hope, which are highly cherished in it. I appreciate the patience of my children – Voke, Oghale, Ajiri and Eloh, and my wife, Dr. (Mrs.) G. E. Ogbimi, who made the house a conducive place for thinking in a very trying time. I am also grateful to Mr. Stephen Eyeh and Mr. Akin Fatokun for being the reading-editors of this book. I thank all other persons whose names are not mentioned here who provided various forms of support or encouragement during the period.

In all situations we ought to give glory to God. As such, it is the Almighty God, the source of life, understanding, wisdom and knowledge that all the glory must be given for the gift of this series.

CONTENTS

1

INTRODUCTION

Beginning in the 1950s some nations of the world including all African nations, were referred to as developing nations or Third World Nations (TWNs), whereas most Western and some Eastern nations were referred to as developed nations or Technologically Advanced Nations (TANs). The most distinguishing features for this classification were probably industrialization and related econo-social-political status. While the TWNs were not industrialised poor societies, the TANs were industrialised and rich societies.

The TANs had been enjoying economic boom as from the eighteenth century. The 1950s and 1960s were specifically called the 'Golden Age' of capitalism (Marglin, 1991). The Golden Age was characterized by full employment, high productivity and low inflation. The TWNs have never enjoyed any economic boom characterized by full employment, high productivity and low inflation.

Nigeria, like many other African nations, has been facing the co-existent problems of mass unemployment, low productivity and high inflation for more than twenty years. Nigeria has also been facing the problems of high crime rate, mass poverty, high indebtedness and high debt accumulation tendency, brain drain, decaying infrastructure, others.

During the past thirty years, Nigeria has largely been pretending to educate her youths. This is because Nigeria's efforts in this regard may be likened to that of a water-pump lifting water from a bore-hole into an over-head water tank that is leaking profusely. The pump merely wastes the fuel utilized in the process, and suffers wear and tear in doing the work of lifting water up into the tank. Nigeria like our model water-pump, reluctantly educates her youths in secondary and tertiary institutions and leaves the young graduates to face the frustration of joblessness and careeless life. In a few years after graduating, the youths forget all they had learnt in their institutions and become too confused to have any drive and initiative.

Why are Nigeria and other African nations facing a myriad of economic problems after planning and executing many plans over a period of about five decades? Are Nigeria's economic problems unsolvable?

The Nigerian situation may be likened to the tourist's error at a T-junction. When a tourist makes a left-turn instead of a right-turn at this special point, the more the effort he puts up, the farther away he becomes from his desired destination (Ogbimi, 1992). We recall the injunction, 'think before you act!' It is a good one to heed always but it is doubtful whether it has ever guided Nigeria's planning since 1960 when she gained flag-independence. This may explain why although many Nigerian planning documents since 1960 have many laudable objectives, there is little or nothing to show for them

Many Nigerians believe that unemployment is the most important problem confronting Nigeria today. The incidence of high crime rate in Nigeria, cultism in tertiary institutions, pervasive corruption, prevalent poverty in the nation and other undesirable developments, are believed to be consequences of the mass unemployment problem and the attendant hopelessness.

Mass unemployment has indeed become a global menace today. The Group of seven most industrial nations, the G7, and Russia met in London in February, 1998 and devoted a lot of time to tackling the problem of unemployment in their nations. Britain, host of the meeting said in a background paper to the session that, 'The purpose of this session is to have a frank assessment of the challenges facing G8 economies.' Owning up to difficulties was the first step in finding solutions, Britain remarked and singled out Italy, France and Germany for their particularly poor performance on job creation. Britain, also said that 'it is only when the challenges we face are probably recognized that we can discuss solution.'

G-8 nations have quite different records on employment problems and so they have varied prescriptions for solving the problem. In Italy, Britain revealed, only 50 per cent of the working-age population has a job, while in France and Germany the ratio rises to 60-65 percent. The ratio rises again to about 70 percent in Britain and Canada, and again to about 75 per cent in the United States and Japan.

Russian Labour Minister, Cleg Sysynyey, said that 'while the West is concerned with too few job opportunities, Russia is afraid that its labour market will soon run out of control.' To the United States Treasury Secretary, Robert Robin, the solution to unemployment lies in reform. He said that "As Europe moves forward with economic and monetary union (EMU), it is important that Europe does not lose sight of the need for structural reform" (The Guardian, Feb. 25, 1998: 40).

The International Labour Organisation (ILO) (1998) released a report in the last quarter of 1998 entitled, "Global Employment Trends: The Outlook is Grim." The report said that one billion people would be unemployed in the world in December 1998. It added that with a few exceptions, the employment situation has remained unfavourable in most nations of the world. The United States where unemployment is at its lowest level since early 1990s presents an exceptional situation.

The ILO report claimed that about 60 million young people between the ages of 15 and 24 are in search of work but cannot find jobs. The ILO claimed in the report that the Asian crisis alone which became more apparent mid-year 1998 was expected to add about 10 million new unemployed people to the unemployed queue by December, 1998. In addition, it warned that "Africa's recovery though encouraging should not be a cause for undue optimism." In other words, the unemployment problem has defied all traditional prescriptions. The situation has been worsening since the 1990s as if unemployment has no solution.

We embarked on a curiosity-driven and multidisciplinary research aimed at understanding the present global distribution of wealth and how wealth is created in 1986 in Ile-Ife. Our efforts in this regard have been blessed abundantly.

Confident that our results have great beneficial implications for mankind, we presented some of them in a public lecture series in 1997 in our University, Obafemi Awolowo University, Ile-Ife, Nigeria. The period beginning from late 1996 through 1998, was also devoted to circulating some of our results among individuals, institutions and governments in Nigeria, other nations of Africa, Europe, America and Asia. In continuation of our efforts to popularize our research results and ensure that they return happiness to the face of mankind, we decided to publish a book series to enable many more people become familiar with our results and their implications.

We are aware that all governments need help. Contrary to the common belief among Nigerians that we need to wait to have the great leader (Mr. GL), Mr. GL is indeed an elusive person. He really does not exist as such. No single individual builds a nation. It is the sum of the many small leadership qualities in virtually every man or woman that builds a nation. This is why in progressive nations, the citizens always discuss their problems, mobilize others and put forward good proposal for solving problems to their governments.

One of the great rewards for our research efforts in Ile-Ife is our success in propounding a scientific theory for the menace of unemployment. Because we believe that unemployment is probably the most serious economic problem in the word today, this book, "SOLUTION TO MASS UNEMPLOYMENT IN NIGERIA" is No. 1 in the series, *Achieving Rapid Industrialisation and Democratisation in Nigeria*. The objective of this book in particular is to popularize the theories of unemployment and industrialization, and how the theories can be applied to the Nigeria situation as well as those of other nations. It also has the objective of encouraging the sharing of ideas about the relationships among industrialization, employment and productivity and wealth creation.

Our research revealed that there cannot be solution to mass unemployment without a rapid industrialization process; hence the sub-title of the book is: *Prompting Accelerated Industrialisation Through Linking Education and Production.*

Let us discuss our key economic problem so that we can understand its nature, its cause and solution. Mankind can only solve the problems he understands.

This is the third printing of this book in about eight years. The printing of new editions is being done speedily to ensure that dated issues are dropped and new issues about economic development are addressed promptly. Issues emphasized/added to this editon are understanding the relationship between national productivity and level of self-employment and the role of employement in national development. Other issues addressed are: how to develop the small and medium scale enterprises (SMEs) in Nigeria and promoting rapid capability-building agricultural development in Nigeria.

This book has eleven main parts in it. These are: (1) Introduction; (2) Why there is mass unemployment in Nigeria; (3) Basis for industrialisation; (4) The Wealth creating cycle; (5) Fruits of industrialisation; (6) Theory of learning, employment, automation, productivity and inflation; (7) The nature of the skill acquisition process; (8) Linking education and production; (9) Mobilizing resources for industrialization; (10) Lessons of history; and (11) Concerted efforts needed. The introductory section having been discussed, the basis of the mass unemployment in Nigeria would now be presented.

2

WHY THERE IS MASS UNEMPLOYMENTIN NIGERIA

There are many reasons why Nigeria and other African nations are experiencing mass unemployment and the attendant low productivity problems. We may group these causes into the following categories: factors related to the backward state of the economy; poor perception of the relationship between national productivity and level of self employment/entrepreneurship; inappropriate perception of the nature of unemployment and its relevance to development; faulty planning premises (theory) and framework (approach); inappropriate economic philosophy; inappropriate development strategies, and inappropriate development activities.

Backward State of Economy

The Nigerian economy is a primitive one. It is an artisan economy in which the fundamental production tools remain hoe, axe, cutlass, etc., and production depends on the energy stored in muscles. Total employment in an artisan economy is usually very small and its ability to absorb highly educated people has traditionally been low. But as an artisan economy is transformed into an industrialized one, the production base expands and the manpower absorptive power increases as well as the total employment. In general, pre-industrial societies experience mass unemployment and low productivity but industrialization solves these problems. Britain, experienced mass unemployment and low productivity for centuries, but these problems apparently vanished as from late eighteenth century when she achieved the first modern Industrial Revolution (Trevelyan, 1948). This means that it is rapid industrialisation that must be stimulated to solve the mass unemployment and low productivity problems confronting Nigeria and other African nations. Any strategy that is not geared toward promoting industrialisation cannot be a fundamental effort toward solving unemployment problem.

Poor Perception of the Relationship Between National Productivit/Poverty and Self-employment/Entrepreneurship

The economic situation in Africa has been worsening since the 1980s. The World Bank in September 2006, said that the poverty situation in Africa is a tragedy. The President of the bank, Mr. Paul Wolfowitz in a press conference at the World Bank Annual Meeting in Singapore, said, "I believe that sub-Saharan Africa has to be the first priority because in this 25 years when 400 million people have escaped poverty, 600 million people in sub-Saharan Africa have been going backward. That is a tragedy for the individuals and it is an unheathy trend for the world as a whole." He also said that after visits to some ten African states, he could appreciate the enormity of the challenges facing the continent and that there was the need for urgent measures to redress the situation (See *The Punch*, Saturday, Septemeber 16, 2006, p.8).

Attendant to prevalent poverty in Africa is mass unemployment of all categories of labour. The International Labour Organisation (ILO) global economic report (2006), said that global unemployment hit a record high of 192 million in year 2005, with young people making up nearly 50 per cent of the jobless.

Yet, not the ILO or any other international organisation relates the poverty in Africa to the mass unemployment and low productivity in the continent. To the ILO - a labour organisation, the parlous state of the global economy in 2005 was the result of unimplemented budget coupled with extra-budgetrary expenses and general lack of fiscal discipline.

In Africa where leaders see the unemployed as politically dangerous, it is better to blame the educational sector for it. If the educational institutions produce graduate youths (15-25 years old) who can immediately employ themselves and others, then, the politically dangerous people would not be there.

In Nigeria, mass unemployment has been co-existing with the worsening poverty situation for decades. Government's solution to the co-existent problems of mass unemployment and poverty is self-employment; government agencies have been providing entrepreneurial training for youth so that they can employ themselves. This explains why the National Directorate of Employment (NDE) was established in 1986. It is obvious that NDE entrepreneural activities have not produced the needed results.

The Obasanjo administration which began in May 1999 had to make it clear that it has adopted self-employment as a policy. Dr. Hassan Lawal, the Labour and Productivity Minister, declared that self-employment is the best option for youths. He made the declaration while opening an Entrepreneurship Development Programme organised by the NDE for 2004 Batch B members of the National Youth Service Corps (NYSC), in Abuja in September 2004. He said, *I wish to remind you that from now onwards, your future lies in your hands*. To the Minister, there is no need to find out any relationship between unemployment and poverty. It is not part of the demands for managing the economy to understand why mass unemployment and prevalent poverty are co-existing. How can such government succeed in solving the problems it does not care to understand.

In line with government thinking that self-employment and entrepreneurship are the solution to mass unemployment and pverty, government through the agency supervising universities - The National Universitities Commission (NUC), has directed that all universities should teach entrepreneurial skills to all university students so that they can employ themselves on graduating.

The duty of a good academic, however, is to provide the information to guide national development. This he does, if only he is able to carry out objective and scientific analyses of the problems of society with a view to finding out the true relationships among concepts, things, issues and problems.

It appears that the main function of those in many international organisations and in governments in many developing nations for many decades so far, has been to deceive the ordinary people that the common problems confronting the developing nations of today have no solutions. The truth however, is that there is nothing new under the sun - the problems have solutions. The claim that self-employment and entrepreneurship are the solutions to mass unemployment and poverty is one important example of the series of fallacious claims that international organisations and governments in Africa have sustained to deceive Africans for decades.

The International Labour Organisation, ILO (1991), conducted a study on the relationship between national productivity and the level of self-employment (LOSE). The study revealed that in the highly productive nations like the United States and Britain, LOSE was about 9 per cent. In the Newly Industrialising Countries like Taiwan, Singapore, South Korea, and Malaysia, LOSE was about 25 per cent. However, LOSE was about 50 per cent in low-productivity and poor nations in Africa, Latin America and Asia. The results of the study show that national productivity is inversely related to LOSE. This generalised statement may be illustrated as in figure 1. The observed trend suggests that LOSE must be reduced in the developing nations to improve national productivity. That is, entrepreneurship and self-employment must be reduced through the encouragement of association and group work to improve natioanl productivity. What is the explanation for the observed trend? It is simple. Self-employment and entrepreneurship-based enterprises are atomized or individualistic work settings. When individuals produce on their own, total production is lower than when the people of a nation work in large groups. Large groups enjoy linkage effects, or economies of scale, using the economists' terminology. Individualistic/atomized production like self-employment and entrepreneurship lead to low total production because they do not enjoy linkage effects or economies of scale.

Nature's lesson in relation to individual and group work is quite instructive. The single silk-thread which the spider spins is a relatively weak structural material which fails under any stress regime. However, the web which the spider makes by combining many of the weak silk-threads, is a potent tool which catches many small creatures on which the spider feeds (Ogbimi, 1999). Again, the single (individual) spider's thread is weak while the web or group of threads is stong.

Adam Smith (1776), also demonstrated that group efforts improve productivity significantly. He observed that making the straight flat-head, sharp-end pin involves 18 steps. When an individual carried out all the operations, the person produced 20 pins per day. However, when 10 people were employed to share the operations, they produced 48,000 (forty-eight thousand) pins in a day, an average of 4,800 pin per person per day. Working in groups and specialisation improved productivity 240 times.

Those who have been sustaining the claim that self-employment and entrepreneurship are the solutions to the mass unemployment and poverty problems in Nigeria either do not know that they are not solutions, or they have been trying to deceive ignorant people and frustrate development in the developing world especially Africa. Those who have been sustaining the fallacious claim failed to realise that the pre-industrialised and poor nations have too high levels of self-employment and entrepreneurship. In the artisans/craftsmen agricultural and poverty-striken African economies, most of the people are either self-employed or they are entrepreneurs. Most of the people are self-employed farmers. Smaller proportions are either traders or artisans/seamstress, motor mechanics, vulcanizers, welders, electricians, radio/television repairers, etc. These are all self-employed entrepreneurs. Why should anyone not be able to see that self-employment and entrepreneurship are the cardinal features of the poverty-striken nations and regions of the world? Why should anyone not realise that these cardinal poverty-related features must be replaced with wealth creating features to improve the quality of life in Africa? Self-employment and entrepreneurship are no solutions to unemployment and poverty problems, because self-employment decreases national productivity and increases poverty.

Poor Perception of the Relationship Between Employment and the Health of Economy

Figure 2 represents Western perception of the problem of unemployment. To Westerners, unemployment is a problem which manpower developers (educational/

National Productivity

Level of Self- Employment (LOSE)

Figure 1:   A Schematic representation of the inverse relationship between National Productivity and the level of self-employment (LOSE)

learning institutions) and population growth worsen. Death reduces unemployment problems. Employers of labour employ labour if they think they would make profit through the employment. In other words, employment is a by-product of profit-making and a supply-demand relationship. To Westerners, unemployment indeed is a social problem which governments may be kind to solve. Thus, Keynes (1936) theorized that persistent unemployment is caused by insufficient demand for goods. Therefore, government even through deficit financing could stimulate demand and the use of underutilized resources and reduce unemployment.

With the problem of unemployment reduced to a mere social problem which governments may be kind to solve through deficit budgeting, there is nothing compelling in maintaining the erstwhile wise policy of full employment and seeing unemployment as a serious economic problem. However, governments quickly recognized that the Keynesian theory provided them opportunities for indiscriminate and frivolous expenditure. Most government began to spend big sums of money on military projects and abandoned the old tradition of balanced budgeting. Inflation and stagnation resulted.

As nations began to experience inflation, Phillips (1958), proposed that the Keynesian theory was also applicable to inflation problem. Phillips theorized that there is a trade-off relationship between inflation and unemployment; increase unemployment if you want to reduce inflation. This relationship became known as the "Phillips' curve." Figure 3 illustrates this relationship. This remains the economists', including World Bank and the International Monetary Fund (IMF) panacea for inflation.

Westerners do not believe that employment and unemployment have any relationship with sustainable economic growth, productivity, industrialization, or the health of an economy as a whole. But we shall see later that the health of an economy is dependent on the level of employment – (in quantity and quality). This in turn determines the level of productivity and inflation in an economy. Hence, Phillips' theory is incorrect and misleading in planning for true growth.

Today, most nations of the world are facing the co-existent problems of low productivity, high unemployment and high inflation, otherwise stagflation. Both the Keynesian theory and its extension by Phillips understandably, are unable to address these problems.

African intellectuals including Nigerian intellectuals, hitherto, had no theories of their own in relation to stagflation. Economic activities in Africa have always been determined by the theories of the West. The situation remains the same. Most African intellectuals probably still have not realized that the pre-industrial societies of Africa and the post-industrial societies in the West cannot be managed in the same way. This situation has been an obstacle to solving the problems of lack of industrialisation, mass unemployment, low productivity, high inflation and poverty that have been facing Nigeria and other African nations for decades.

Faulty Planning Theory and Framework

Okigbo (1989), analysed the Nigerian planning process 1900-1992 and noted that the theory that guided the Nigerian First National Plan 1962-68, was the Harrod (1939)–Domar (1946) Model – the HDM, and the model remains Nigeria's planning theory. This model in its simplest form states that the growth in income achievable by a nation depends on the rate of savings and capital invested. In other words, the more the capital invested, the higher would be the growth of income in a society. The HDM assumes that labour is not needed in the production process or that there is only one input in the production process and that is capital (Glabe, 1977).

The classical growth theory of economists as represented by the Cobb-Douglas (1928) aggregate production function, assumes that labour and capital are the principal factors of production, and labour and capital can be substituted for one another in the production process. The HDM is a degenerated form of the classical aggregate production function; it (the HDM) assumes that labour is surplus, hence the limiting factor to improving productivity is capital or that productivity cannot be improved by increasing labour without increasing capital input. The HDM also assumes that capital and labour are perfectly complementary factors and are combined in fixed proportions. How can a nation planning on the premise that capital is the limiting factor to improving productivity solve unemployment problem? Impossible!

Most economists claim that once capital investment is made, growth follows and employment is created. This is not true at all. As we shall show later, capital investment *per se*, cannot stimulate sustainable economic growth. Thus, mere growth of capital does not lead to sustainable economic growth. The UNDP (1997) report showed that Nigeria and some other nations grew without creating new job opportunities in the period covered by the report. The report supports our position that mere increase in capital investments does not automatically lead to sustainable economic growth.

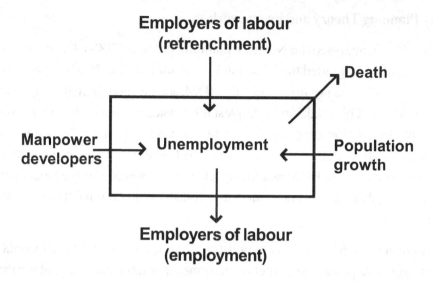

Figure 2: **Western perception of Unemployment problem: A supply - demand relationship.**

The HDM, Rostow's growth theory (1960) and others like them constitute the modernization theories. These are efforts of the World Bank, the International Monetary Fund (IMF), and their social scientists friends to operationalise the evolutionary and neo-evolutionary theories. The evolutionary and modernization theories are mechanistic and ahistorical perception of the human development experience (Hoogvelt, 1976). There are many contributors to the evolutionary theories. August Comte, William Summer, William Spencer and Vilfredo Pareto were major evolutionists, while Ferdinand Tonnies, Emile Durkheim, Max Weber, and Talcot Parson, were major neo-evolutionists.

They claimed that Western Europe in the sixteenth century had achieved the maximum level of development for human societies. The authors then classified nations into two categories – Simple (primitive) or Complex (advanced). African and Latin American nations were classified as the primitive ones, whereas nations in the West were classified as the advanced ones. The evolutionists and modernists then proposed that primitive people and places may be made modern by transferring

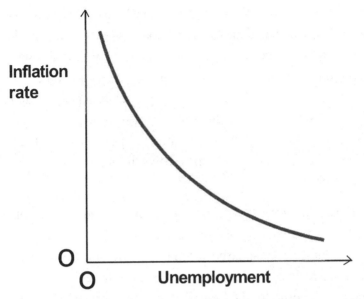

Figure 3 :   The Phillips' curve
Source: Phillips (1958).

resources especially technology from the rich West to them. This is the origin of International Technology Transfer (ITT) in its various forms as the main development strategy for Nigeria and other African nations.

In a society where capital is seen as the most important factor of production, planning is synonymous with efforts towards making capital available (Galbraith, 1967). Nigeria has existed for about five decades, operating based on the principle that capital is the most important factor of production, not manpower resources. This is clearly reflected in: (i) the 5-year national plans (1962-1985) and the 3-year rolling plans since the adoption of the Structural Adjustment Programmes (SAPs) in 1986; (ii) relationships among government ministries and personnel relationships; (iii) utterances of government officials in matters related to managing the economy; and (iv) utterances of influential people in the private sector and the position of influential Nigerian intellectuals.

For the First National Plan 1962-68, the thinking which guided the activities was that the average growth rate of the National economy during the period 1950-60 was estimated to be 3.9 per-cent per annum. Based on this estimate, it was predicted that the investment of 15 per cent of the Gross Domestic Product (GDP) would raise per capital consumption by 1 per-cent per year and Nigeria would achieve self-sustaining growth by merely raising the domestic saving ratio from 9.5 per cent of GDP in 1960-61 to about 15 per cent or higher by 1975. This thinking was based on the HDM and the belief that industrialisation is achieved through mere capital investment.

From the earliest time, government ministries in Nigeria had a power-relationship structure that made the Ministry of Finance the center of decision in government. The Ministry of Finance has since been combining multiple functions, including national planning and determining industrialisation strategies. The Minister of Finance and the Governor of the Central Bank of Nigeria (CBN) are probably the most powerful officials, next in command to the head of government, because they control the release of money. Similarly, the Director of Finance in any particular ministry is more powerful than his counterparts because he decides whether money will be released or not. This is an unfortunate situation. The Vice-President, Finance, in a business organisation for example, does not do the planning for a firm. He sources money for the company and advises on proper financing. He does not determine the project that should be funded by his company; management approves projects.

In a well-structured government, it is the Ministry of National Planning that should coordinate the planning process. Ministry of Finance is only to source and release funds as directed by the National Planning Ministry. The existing set-up in Nigeria in which the Ministry of Finance and Governor of the CBN do the planning for the nation and also determine what to release and when and whom to release money is unfortunate and detrimental to the progress of Nigeria.

The Honourable Minister of Finance, Chief Anthony Ani (1996), said while briefing the press about the 1996 budget that the performance of the economy in 1995 was unsatisfactory due largely to the characteristics of the economy; production must be emphasized to turn things around. The emphasis of the 1996 budget accordingly, included; increasing foreign private investment and foreign reserves, managing interest rates, completing Export Processing Zones (EPZs) to earn increased foreign exchange, among others. He also said that growth induced by investments through privatisation and liberalisation with both domestic and foreign investments will generate job and enable Nigerians acquire new skills. Ani (1997), again having complained about the performance of the economy in 1996 said that the trust of the 1997 budget was to stimulate private investment in the country so as to substantially raise the level of production. The focus he said, was motivated by experience which shows that a high and sustained level of private investment is the only sure way of attaining the level of production needed to assure sustainable growth and development. Whose experience was Chief Ani referring to? Chief Anthony Ani's perception of the development process cited here represents the refrain of the songs that all Nigerian Ministers/Commissioners of Planning, Finance, Industry, others, have been singing since 1960.

Ohiwerei (1998) in his write-up entitled, "Why Nigeria must liberalize," said, that Nigeria must liberalise to achieve sustainable economic growth. The competition for limited financial resources of local and foreign investors, he added, has put pressure on nations to liberalize and create an attractive environment to retain entrepreneurs and attract foreign direct investments. Ohiwerei is a respected industrialist. To Ohiwerei, again, capital investment is the way to stimulate sustainable economic growth.

Ndiokho (1998), another respected industrialist in Nigeria, said, "I think the very thing that is facing Nigeria is creating enabling environment that will allow foreign investors to come and invest." He claimed that creating enabling environment is the vogue today. Since the world has become globalised, Nigeria cannot pretend not to belong to the global community. The truth is that he was indeed advocating the continued application of the HDM in Nigeria.

Adedeji (1993), is a respected Nigerian economist. In his paper entitled, "African and Orthodox Structural Adjustment Programmes: Perception, Policy and Politics," he criticized the orthodox adjustment programmes introduced to African nations by the World Bank and the International Monetary Fund (IMF) for being unsuitable for the region. He suggested an African Alternative Framework, one that is human-centred. But again, his proposition rests on the premise that 'increased production almost invariably results from a greater use of capital inputs' – the HDM.

Today, after implementing SAPs for over 20 years and implementing the National Economic Empowerment and Development Strategy (NEEDS) for four years, the most acclaimed gains are the bank consolidation and increase in foreign reserves - financial gains, with attendant prevalent poverty.

It is clear from the above illustrations that the belief that the more the capital invested the higher is the growth rate achievable, is one held by virtually all groups influencing development planning in Nigeria today. To an individual or group which holds this belief, the availability of employment openings and manpower development are not important to industrialization; they are the fruits of income growth and profit-making. Unfortunately, this is not true. This explains Nigeria's predicament. This also explains why all other nations in Africa are stagnating.

The point here is that those who have been planning for Nigeria since 1960 do not believe that manpower development is essential to achieving sustainable economic growth and industrialisation (SEGI). How could Nigeria achieve her manpower development objectives and solve unemployment problem? Nigeria's thinking as regards industrialisation and solving unemployment problem is faulty. This explains why Nigeria cannot progress in her industrialisation endeavour. This also explains why Nigeria is facing mass unemployment and low productivity problems. For industrialisation expands and diversifies the production base of an economy. This in turn, creates learning and employment opportunities and improves productivity. Growing economies demand employment of all categories (Lewis, 1972).

Correspondingly, stagnating economies face mass unemployment problem. Mass unemployment is the principal symptom of stagnation.

Why has it been possible for Nigeria to adopt a planning premise that does not promote sustainable economic growth and industrialisation for decades? First, it served the interests of those in and close to government. While the nation gets poorer and poorer each year over the years, few people in and close to government have become instantaneous millionaires. Secondly, Nigerians hitherto, lacked independent intellectual postions.

More importantly, the sustenance of the faulty premise is partly made possible by the passive approach to planning during the period. The common planning framework during the period was the rational planning approach. There are six steps in it. These are: Establishing objectives; Establishing planning premise; Determine alternative courses; Evaluate alternatives; Select course of action; and Formulate a derivative plan. In this approach, objectives are set before any attempt to understand the nature of the problems to be solved. This means that beautiful objectives may indeed be set even when those planning for a nation do not understand the nature of the problems they are planning to solve. The objectives set in this approach were best described as non-achievable ones.

Nigeria has quite laudable objectives in virtually all her planning documents since 1960. Examination of all the plans since 1962 show that they all contain beautiful philosophies and objectives. Some of the objectives in the plans among others are: (i) Development of skilled manpower; (ii) Development of agriculture, industry and infrastructure (roads, electricity, water, telecommunication, others); (iii) Provide education, health, employment opportunities and better living standards for all citizens; (iv) Acquire science and technology, diversify and modernize economy, and improve productivity; and (v) Achieve self-reliance and balanced and uniform development. Additional objectives since the advent of the Structural Adjustment Programmes (SAPs) in 1986 are privatization of public enterprises and paying national debts, and solving mass unemployment, prevalent poverty and high crime wave problems.

The development of skilled manpower was especially emphasized in the First National Plan (1962-68). It was lamented that its scarcity in Nigeria at that time was the most important constraint to Nigeria's development. These were all lip-services to non-achievable objectives.

In the scientific Planning Process (Ogbimi and Adjebeng-Asem, 1994), the phases are seven: Problem recognition, Problem perception (or problem conceptualization or understanding), Setting achievable objectives, Plan implementation, Programme monitoring/appraisal, Plan review and Plan termination. A nation only sets achievable objectives, if the people understand the nature of the problems they have to solve. Otherwise, the nation merely conceives wild dreams as objectives while the people erroneously claim that 'the inability to achieve national objectives is a consequence of poor implementation of well formulated policies.'

Many Nigerians (Ilori, 1998; Uga, 1998; and Popoola, 1998) claim that the problem frustrating progress in Nigeria is poor implementation of laudable plans. But this is not true. As it has been shown and will be further demonstrated later, the most serious problem frustrating economic progress in Nigeria is poor perception or understanding of the problems confronting Nigeria. No style of implementation corrects the error of faulty thinking (premise or theory) in the planning process. Implementation is the fourth phase in the Scientific Planning Framework (SPF). Nigeria would have to adopt the SPF and learn to avoid passivity in planning and subject the premise of any new plan to a critical analysis to progress.

Inappropriate Economic Philosophy/Ideology

Many Nigerians are better at swallowing and regurgitating the intellectual positions of Westerners. Nigerians are ideologues. They are either socialists or capitalists. Both the socialist/communist and capitalist economic philosophies unfortunately originated from the West. What then is the fundamental difference between the two economic philosophies referred to as capitalism and socialism/communism?

Fundamentally, there is no difference between the communist and capitalist, particularly as regards their understanding of the human development process. The leader of the communists, Karl Marx (1867) was the first to say that the key feature of the capitalist system is that machinery facilitates a continuous revolutionary and creative production in agriculture and industry, communication and transportation. He also said that the capitalist must accumulate capital to start. In other words, capital is the primary basis of sustainable economic growth. This remains the fundamental basis of development theory in the West. This as we shall show later is not true.

Thus, both the socialist/communist and capitalist perception of the development process is one but wrong. The West did not accumulate capital as a pre-condition before achieving modern Industrial Revolution (Gerschenkron, 1966). This explains why socialist and capitalist governments in Africa have not been able to meet the aspirations of the African people. Although the socialists/communists claim that the objective of the system of governance is to make all the citizens happy and that socialism is cooperation and accused capitalist of pretending to encourage inventions and distribute the benefits in the fairest way attainable, they (socialist/communist) have not been able to demonstrate their position in relation to their societies. The former Union Soviet Socialist Republics (USSR) failed after only about seventy years of existence. Karl Marx predicted that capitalist systems would collapse after a while. Unfortunately, the prediction turned out to be for the communists. The former USSR, the first practical test of the theory of communism collapsed about 1990. The second experiment, China, seems confused today. It seems to have decided to abandon communism and to adopt market-economic principles. This is a consequence of not understanding the nature of the development process.

Capitalism has evolved over six phases (Inman, 1984). These are: Precapitalism, before 1500 A.D.; Mecantile capitalism, 1500-1800; Free capitalism, 1750-1890s; Industrial capitalism, 1860-1920s; Finance capitalism, 1890s-1930;

Regulated capitalism, 1930s-present and Responsive capitalism, 1915-present. Mercantile capitalism and Free capitalism or deregulation were all abandoned in the West before the beginning of the twentieth century. Capitalism had become regulated and its proponents had come to see that business people must be responsive to the needs of the people who allow them to stay and do business in their environment. The elements of capitalism according to Lodge (1977) are: individualism; equal opportunity; private property rights; competition; limited government; and specialization and fragmentation. But Westerners have come to realize that capitalism does not promote common good. Russell (1967), observed that individualism does not promote the growth of scientific knowledge and capabilities, because the growth of these demands a close-knit society; individualism discourages cooperation in a society and frustrates development.

Westerners have, as such, been trying and have indeed converted their societies into welfare states by adopting many socialistic principles. Western governments promote mass education, they pay unemployment allowances to the citizens who have no jobs, they care for the aged, etc. These are all attempts to ameliorate the pains of capitalism.

Lodge (1977a), realized that capitalism is not the ideology of the future and proposed a new one for America. He proposed communitarianism as the ideology to replace capitalism. Lodge reasoned that the community has its own special needs. Individual survival and self-esteem depend upon the recognition and, enlargement of community needs. Personal fulfillment should be achieved by gaining a place in the community. Consequently, rather than stress individualism, the new ideology should emphasise communitarianism. Similarly, the emerging economic philosophy should emphasize equality of results rather than mere equal opportunity, consensus instead of contract, rights of membership instead of property rights, cooperation-community needs instead of competition, active planning government instead of limited government, holistic approach to planning instead of atomistic approach and interdependence instead of the independence which dated capitalism stresses.

In view of the strong evidence suggestive of the need to dump capitalistic economic philosophy in the West, it is now that Africans, including Nigerians, are discovering capitalistic principles as the panacea to African problems. Consequently, Africans have been talking of privatization (extreme individualism), Free capitalism (deregulation or planlessness or market forces or *laissez-faire* economics) for decades now. Westerners abandoned individualism and market forces in the nineteenth century. If free market capitalism were the panacea economic philosophy why did Westerners abandon it?

Africans are also being urged to return to mercantile capitalism under the cover of the new phraseology called globalization. Globalization is the result of improvements in computer and communication technologies which have made communication much easier than hitherto, and reduced the world to a small village. How does this development change the African economic status? Has it improve or worsened it? What is Africa's contribution to globalization?

The economic status of a nation in the world has become well known to be highly dependent on its technological status – its ability to use scientific knowledge to solve problems, including production. The growth of technology has made it possible for many Americans to engage in industrial, commercial and service occupations and to make the United States the most powerful nation in the world *(Bulletin of Science, Technology & Society,* 1984). When two societies produce different goods and become involved in mutual exchange of the goods (trading), then, we have interdependence. In this situation, learning and employment opportunities would develop mutually in each nation from production and trading activities. But when only one society (A) is able to produce the needs of the other (B), while the other (B), is unable to produce its own needs and for the other society (A), or when one (B) only produces the goods that other societies (A, C) are able to manipulate the prices, we have an unfair economic relationship. This is what mercantile capitalism in the West, 1500-1800 A.D., was.

Mercantile capitalists believed that the nation must maintain self-sufficiency by producing its own food and manufacturing its own articles. Mercantilists also advocated that the nation must establish colonies; the colonial system was to enable the nation to secure necessary raw materials and absorb surpluses of manufactured goods produced by the mercantile mother nation, while all development aspirations are suppressed. The American colonies were a direct result of the English mercantile policy (Inman, 1984). How is the relationship between Africa and the West different from a mercantile one today?

The manufacturing sectors of African economies continue to show slow progress (African Development Bank, 1997). The average contribution of the manufacturing sector to total GDP in Africa in 1996 was less than 12 per cent. During the past decade, Africa's share in world Manufacturing Value Added (MVA), remained blow 1 (one) per cent. Africa's share of World MVA in apparel is less than 1 (one) percent. African share of the global economy in 1958 was 15.6 per cent; the share had dropped to 2.1 per cent in 2006 (World Bank and IMF, 2006).

The World Bank issued a statement during its 1998 meeting with the IMF in Washington lamenting, that Africa is losing $68 billion a year in export, due to declining share of world trade (*The Guardian*, 1998). Africa's share of world trade had dropped from 3 per cent in the 1960s to less than 2 per cent in the 1990s, the statement added. Continuing, the bank noted the fact that Africa's export had grown from a rate of four per cent between 1975 to 1984 to 7.9 per cent in 1996. The bank was of the view that the lack of impact of the growth of export suggested that Africa's rate of growth of export had not kept pace with rates in other regions. Africa's export the statement also said, had been dominated by primary commodities in agriculture, mineral and metals. Primary products accounted for 60 per cent in Africa's export compared to 33 per cent for all developing nations. Unfortunately, the statement lamented, industrialized nations are yet to open their markets to African nations, especially to the vital agricultural products, textiles and clothing.

How does the present economic strength and status of Africa, including Nigeria prepare Africa to compete as an economic block among other blocks in the world? How does globalization, especially, enhance the competitive strength of Africa?

Competitive advantage is not something which falls from heaven like manna; it is created and earned (Ormerod, 1994).

William Daley (1998), American Commerce Secretary, visited South Africa late in 1998. While delivering a keynote address at the International Herald Tribune's two-day Southern African Trade and Investment Summit which began in Cape Town on December 1, 1998, he revealed the relative self-reliance indices of some of the world's economic blocks. He stated that only 13 percent of African trade is with other African countries in contrast to Europe where 68 percent trade is with other European nations and Asia where 30 percent trade is within the continent. How does globalisation change these fundamentals? African leaders have been attending meetings for decades to form economic blocks. Where is the basis when there is little or no production within the continent? Where is the basis for learning and employment opportunities in the continent, including Nigeria, when there are virtually no production and trade activities within the continent?

Blind adoption of ideologies or economic philosophies would not save African nations, including Nigeria. Nigeria must abandon frivolous concepts like deregulation, market forces, market economy, privatization, etc., to face the realities of today. Africa or any other economic block cannot increase the trading within it without increasing the production strength first. The commodity for a trade must exist before the trade based on it.

Inappropriate Development Strategies and Activities

Nigeria's main development strategy and activities have all been related to International Technology Transfer (ITT). ITT again, is an attempt to operationalise the modernization theories which claim that the primitive people and places in Africa and other continents may be made modern by transferring resources, especially technology and capital from the advanced and modern West to them.

The ITT development strategy has many forms today. Girvan (1983) identified ten of these as:

(i)   Foreign direct investment;

(ii)   Licensing for production;

(iii)   Contractual supply of management-related technology;

(iv)   Sale and installation of 'turnkey' plants;

(v)   Procurement of machinery;

(vi)   Design and construction of infrastructure and buildings;

(vii)   Engineering and feasibility consultancy;

(viii) Technical assistance and advice;

(ix)   Training of personnel at home and abroad; and

(x)   Individual acquisition of knowledge.

To these we can add the more familiar and recent popular strategies such as:

-     Import Substitution Industrialisation,
-     Appropriate Technology Industrialisation.
-     Foreign Aid-led Industrialisation.
-     Private Sector-led Industrialisation,
-     Agriculture-led Industrialisation,
-     Export-led Industrialisation,
-     Globalization and Information Technology,
-     Self-employment/cooperative programmes,
-     Others.

Associated with the above strategies and programmes over the years in Nigeria are activities such as:

-     Mass and indiscriminate importation;
-     Indiscriminate and reckless award of highly inflated contracts and receipt of kickbacks;
-     Indiscriminate erection of structures (road and communication networks, industrial estates, iron and steel plants, aluminum smelting plants, Liquefied Natural Gas (LNG) plants, petrochemical plants, refineries, airports, seaports, dams, irrigation networks, water treatment plants, educational systems, Export

Processing zones (EPZs), etc.;

- Indiscriminate expansion of the financial system (the banking and insurance industry and the capital market);
- Fly-in experts project (the UNDP project coded TOKTEN - Transfer of Knowledge Through Expatriate Nationals);
- Indiscriminate currency devaluation;
- The Structural Adjustment Programmes and the associated Foreign Exchange Market (FEM) – the mandatory devaluation instrument.

Girvan (1983), also observed that the term, *transfer of technology* commonly found in development policy and technology policy literature is used to refer to activities such as the construction of irrigation or hydro-electric work by foreign contractors. It is also used to refer to the installation of a manufacturing facility by a foreign company, or the production of a manufactured product by a local enterprise under license from a foreign company.

Vaitos (1975), noted that the term *transfer* represents a rather loose usage of the word, or it could be an indication of insufficient knowledge of the phenomena involved or it could be grouped as part of what Myrdal called *diplomacy by terminology*. He prefers the term commercialisation of technology, indicating not only that a commercial transaction takes place, but also that the characteristics of the market for the transactions and the nature of technology itself are such that the sellers possess enormous bargaining power.

Examination of the history of technological development experiences over the period 3000 B.C. – present (Ogbimi, 1996), revealed that the commercialisation of human development interactions is quite recent. There was no terminology like *technology transfer* before the second half of the twentieth century.

Egwaikhide (1997), reviewed Nigeria's import substitution development strategy and its implementation. He found out that the strategy depleted and aggravated Nigeria's problem of balance of payments, because it demanded increased foreign inputs, technology and expertise for production. Onimode (1982), found out that the employment -generating ability of the import substitution industrialisation strategy is negligible.

Thus, Nigeria has been wasting time and other resources pursuing ITT for decades. ITT cannot promote industrialization and ITT cannot generate learning and employment opportunities because it is a passive, corruption-and-poverty promoting process, whereas achieving sustainable growth and industrialisation is a very active learning and disciplining process.

3

BASIS FOR INDUSTRIALISATION

We have demonstrated that Nigeria's thinking, strategy and activities related to development over the past decades have not been the types that promote sustainable economic growth and industrialisation. Nor were they those that create learning and employment opportunities. How then could Nigeria have promoted rapid industrialisation? Again, the thinking and activities of a society with respect to promoting industrialisation must be right if the society is to achieve rapid industrialisation. We shall now discuss what right thinking about industrialisation entails.

Right Thinking About Industrialisation

The comparative analysis of the economic statuses of the non-industrialised nations and the industrialised ones can be depicted on a competence-scale. Whereas the non-industrialised artisans/craftsmen nations in Africa have very low competence and produce mainly agricultral goods, the industrialised Western and Asian nations have very high competence (capabilities) and produce both agricultural and manufactured/ engineered goods. Using the y-axis as the competence-scale, the position of the non-industrialised nations may be marked as point A (low competence) while the position of the industrialised may be marked as point B (high competence) above point A. Industrialisation may then be defined in relation to the model-scale as a progression from point A towards point B. The issue under examination now is: What do nations do to promote rapid industrialisation? What do nations do to move up rapidly on the competence-scale?

Capital investment cannot stimulate growth: A Theory

Capital investment, per se, does not stimulate sustainable economic growth (Ogbimi, 1997). Capital investments may erect structures, including industrial plants, but they do not increase competence (the ability to do things, including,

29

production), instantaneously. Competence is not a commodity that can be bought or increased instantaneously when a critical value is lacking (Brautaset, 1990). Nigeria's inability to manufacture modern goods is due to the absence of the Relevant Production Skills, RPSs (Ogbimi, 1992a). Unfortunately, Nigeria cannot purchase the RPSs through capital investment. This is what is demonstrated here.

Africans are aware that whereas European nations, America and Japan are industrialised and manufacture many goods, African nations are only involved in artisan/craft agriculture and are unable to produced manufactured or engineered goods. To change the unhappy situation where all African nations import all the manufactured and luxury goods they consume, African nations have been involved in International Technology Transfer for many decades. African nations have been begging Western nations for Foreign Direct Investments (FDIs) in Africa; Africans have been erecting industrial plants themselves. The shameful and endless campaign by all African leaders is based on the belief that as investments flow into Africa, a time would come when enough FDIs would have assembled all types of industrial plants in Africa and the continent would achieve industrialisation and begin to produce many manufactured goods like European nations, America, Canada and Japan have been doing for centuries.

African nations import very many things and erect many structures - road and telecommunication networks, industrial plants, urban centers, real estate, airport and sea-ports, stadia, air-planes, railways, etc., to modernise Africa. African nations have been importing tractors to improve agricultural productivity. These efforts have continued for decades to no avail. Africa is much worse off today than it was in the 1970s. Africa is also much poorer and hopeless. Virtually all African nations have become highly indebted. What is happening? Why can African nations not achieve their objective of achieving industrialization and producing manufactured goods through ITT?

When a technologically backward nation imports a machine and builds a road, it merely acquires Depreciating Assets (DAs). A machine, industrial plant and road, are all DAs because their value depreciate with time and usage even with maintenance. Therefore, FDIs and importation accumulate DAs.

Depreciation is a well-known concept to all persons, especially economists, accountants and business managers. There are many approaches to doing depreciation. The straight line depreciation approach is popular. This approach can be stated in the form of the equation (Ogbimi, 1997):

$$V_t = V_0 - Kt \dots \dots \dots \dots \quad (1)$$

where V_t is the value of the asset at time, $t = 0, 1, 2 \dots \dots \dots \dots$; V_0 is the initial value of the asset; and K is the annual depreciation constant.

For one who acquires a machine for production, equation (1) may be interpreted in a slightly different manner. In this case, V_t is better described as the production strength at time, $t = 0, 1, 2$---; V_0 is the initial production strength; and K is the reduction in production strength every year till the machine is abandoned. Equation (1) is an expression of a real situation or natural occurrence; it is a scientific statement of a natural process. In the traditional way accountants do depreciation, if an asset is purchased for ₦500,000 and it is to be depreciated over five years, the asset is depreciated N500,000) 5 years or ₦100,000 per year. At the end of the first year of usage, the residual amount or the worth of the asset becomes ₦500,000 – ₦100,000 or ₦400,000. At the end of the second year of usage, the worth of the asset becomes ₦400,000 – ₦100,000 or ₦300,000. At the end of the fifth year of usage, the worth of the asset in the books becomes zero.

The same values would be obtained when the appropriate values are substituted in equation (1). In the equation, the period over which the asset would be depreciated is consider as the maximum time in the equation, t_{max}; the amount the asset is purchased is V_0; and $K = V_0$) t_{mas}.

When the values of the asset are plotted against time – 0, 1, 2 .., 5, the results would be like the illustration in figure 4. The illustration shows that just as the value of the depreciating asset decreases, so the production strength decreases with time and usage. We can conclude that capital investment per se, whether domestic or foreign, and whether direct or through the capital market (equity subscription) does not promote sustainable growth.

Our scientific expression of the nature of structures may also be analyzed algebraically. In this circumstance, equation (1) may be called the value-time function for the DA. The equation may also be called the depreciation equation of the DA. It is a decreasing function which shows that the production strength of a society that emphasizes capital investment decreases with time.
Thus, $V_1 = V_0 - K$, for t = 1; $V_2 = V_0 - 2K$, for t = 2; etc.

Applying the *concept of limits* in mathematics to equation (1), we have that:

$$\text{As } t \to t_{max}, \; Kt \to V_0, \text{ and } V_t \to 0$$

where t_{max} is the average service-life of the structure. This means that as a developing nation emphasizes capital investment and builds structures, the structures immediately begin to depreciate in value with increasing usage and age till the structures cannot render the service for which they were acquired and they are abandoned. The development of maintenance capabilities will reduce the depreciation rate, but it would not change the nature of structures – they are DAs. Achieving sustainable economic growth each year, demands that the production strength of the society should increase each year. But the economy of the capital-emphasizing developing nation goes through the stress fluctuating cycle of accumulation (or acquisition) – depreciation, accumulation-depreciation – a saw-tooth wave, without achieving sustainable economic growth. The nation therefore suffers perpetually, increasing stress of trying to restore the value of depreciated assets in attempt to sustain them in service. The cumulative Value Restoring Stress (S_c) from equation (1) is:

$$S_c = Kt \; \dots\dots\dots\dots\dots\dots\dots\dots\dots\dots\dots \quad (2)$$
$$\text{for } t = 1, 2, \dots, n$$
$$S_c = K, \text{ for } t = 1$$
$$= 2K, \text{ for } t = 2$$
$$= nK, \text{ for } t = n$$

S_c is the pain suffered by a technologically backward nation for attempting to build the roof of a house before laying the foundation.

A backward economy emphasizing capital investment may be likened to a blood-cancer patient. This patient unlike the healthy person, does not produce blood cells (life-sustaining requirement) and depends on external supply (blood transfusion) for his requirement of blood cells. The import-dependent society also depends on external supply (import) for its essential requirements (machinery and equipment, raw materials, food, etc.). The import-dependent economy and the blood-cancer patient are therefore very sick systems which do not have long-term plans. This explains the perpetually bad state of the Nigerian economy and the bad state of the industrial plants (refineries, iron and steel plants) and the infrastructure in particular. No amount of investment *per se*, can improve the state of the Nigerian economy; only industrialisation would solve the problem of decaying structures. Those who complain about the bad state of Nigerian infrastructure are mischievous; the complex infrastructure erected through inflated contracts in an artisan economy will perpetually be in a bad state.

A graphical illustration of equation (1) is shown in figure 5. The (a) portion shows the trend of the production strength of an economy which emphasizes capital investment; it decreases perpetually. The (b) portion

(a) **Mathematical (demonstrably)**

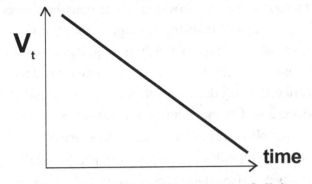

(b) **Phenomenologically (wonderfully)**

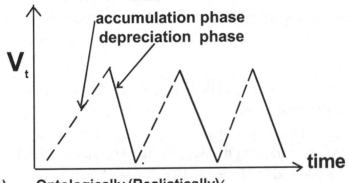

(c) **Ontologically (Realistically)**

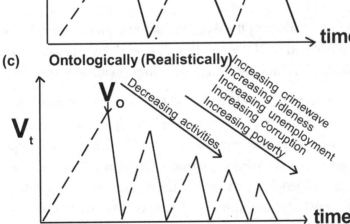

Figure 5 : Graphical illustration of the variation of the wealth creating potential, V_t of the capital investment - emphasizing society.

is a phenomenological analysis of the activities in a technologically backward nation pursuing ITT development strategy; it shows the fluctuations that the economy of the import-dependent and capital investment-emphasizing nation experiences without achieving Sustainable Economic Growth and Industrialization (SEGI). The (c) portion of the figure illustrates the more practical situation; it suggests that economic activities in the economy decrease with time as the values of the structures (depreciating assets) decrease. Correspondingly, passivity, idleness, unemployment, poverty, corruption, indiscipline, crime waves, indebtedness and other evils increase till the economy collapses. Our illustration quite matched Nigeria's experience since 1960. It also aptly described the situation in other African nations. Those who shamelessly beg for foreign investments are the promoters of passivity, speculation, poverty and corruption in Africa. Those who are encouraging Nigeria and the other African nations to pursue ITT are the people trying to ruin the hope of all Africans.

The United Nations Development Programme (UNDP) Human Development Reports (since 1990) have persistently painted the sad situation of growing and pervasive poverty in Nigeria. The Structural Adjustment Programmes (SAPs) introduced to African nations by the World Bank and the International Monetary Fund (IMF) was adopted by Nigeria in 1986, some 21 (twenty-one) years ago. Why is it that Nigeria is collapsing decades after implementing SAPs?

Contrary to the claims by the World Bank and IMF on one hand and their friends in Nigeria on the other hand that the programme is poorly implemented, SAPs are not a development programme, rather they are punitive measures supposedly designed to achieve many wild dreams, (better called non-achievable objectives) like those in all other Nigeria's national plans. The original document (Bello, 1987), showed unambiguously that the primary objective of SAPs was to enable Nigeria pay her questionable foreign and local debts. SAPs could not even achieve this objective. National debts are cumulative effects of mismanagement. Progressive nations pay debts whereas retrogressing nations cannot pay their debts.

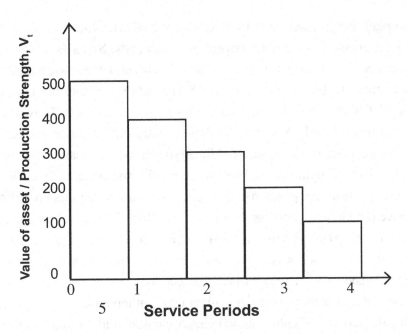

**Figure 4: The change in the value of capital asset
due to usage and aging.**

SAPs are unable and cannot achieve any objective because of the faulty thinking (theory) underlying them. Again, no implementation style corrects the faulty error of thinking in the planning process. The world Bank and IMF merely perceived the Nigerian problem as one of mismatch between supply and demand of Nigeria's needs. To the Brentton Woods-economists, Nigeria was importing more than she can pay for; it is a demand-management problem (Quarcoo, 1990). Solution: reduce import (demand). How? Increase cost of imports through mandatory devaluation of the Naira using the instrument of the Foreign Exchange Market (FEM), and reduce government expenditure on social welfare (through reduced allocation, privatisation, commerciation of educational institutions, health systems, retrenchment, others), so that Nigeria can pay her debts.

Nigeria's planning premise since 1960 remains the HDM, which lacks growth-promoting elements, but promotes poverty and other evils. SAPs did not change the premise. SAPs however worsened the situation because they have additional peculiar features. Ogbimi (1997), analyzed SAPs and showed that they have the sad effect of dismantling both advanced and developing economies. They do this quite rapidly through the FEMs. First, SAPs were designed to increase speculation in all African economies. Consequently African youths both illiterate and educated, are now involved in buying and selling various articles and using motor cycles to transport people from one position to another so as to earn money quickly. Youths do not have time to learn and use their hands anymore. This key learning and development group has been dismantled by SAP. Second, the sudden increase in the cost of imports has serious deleterious effects on the production linkages in an economy. Consider the Nigerian artisan/craft economy, the artisan - mechanics, electricians, panel beaters/painters, vulcanizers, others, are the key people sustaining the economy. With a saloon Peugeot car now sold for about 3 (three) million naira, no individual buys a new car in Nigeria. With wages much below subsistence level, those who have old cars cannot afford to buy spare parts to service them. Hence, the artisan has little or no patronage. With no patronage, the artisans who have been trying to understand the functioning and making of the products Nigeria imports, had to abandon their workshops to return to farms or stay idle in motor parks or join criminals, contributing much less or negatively to the growth of the Nigerian economy. This illustration shows how SAPs dismantle linkages and weaken economies when it is adopted. Third, SAP is not a development programme, it is a punitive one. History confirms this. Germany's experience is pertinent here.

At the end of the World War I in 1914, the Allied powers (the United States, Britain, France, and Russia), the victors, subjected Germany to what may be called German-SAPs, so that she can pay them war reparations which the victors estimated to be US $33 billion (Stolper, 1967 and Glahe, 1977). One dollar, exchanged 4.2 marks in 1914 before the war. One year into the European SAPs in 1920, one dollar exchange for 63 marks. In 1921, 200 marks exchanged for one dollar. In 1922, 2000 (two thousand) marks exchanged for one dollar. In 1923, the mark as money collapsed, 4.2 trillion marks exchanged for one dollar. Every German was impoverished and disgraced.

The imposed hardship probably set the stage for World War II. Lord Maynard Keynes had indeed warned that the Versaille's Treaty which had the European SAPs as part of it would probably cause another World War. He left the negotiating team when his warning was ignored. The rapid depreciation of the German mark which ensued in view of the production strength of the German economy before it was subjected to SAP is another testimony to the strong dismantling effect of SAPs on any economy.

The Germans knew that SAPs were punitive measure to which they were subjected by the Allied powers. When the hyperinflation ended in November 1923, price level had risen by a factor of 1.02×10^{10} and money supply had increased by about 7.32×10^9 times (Cagan, 1956). The punitive, mandatory devaluation was halted by the commissioner for National Currency, Hjalmer Horace Greecy Schact who promptly stopped printing the mark and issued a new currency (the Rent-mark) that was equal to one trillion old mark.

Nigerians who are waiting for the naira to appreciate say so because of ignorance, for there is no basis for appreciation of the local currency in the mandatory devaluation setting. African SAPs are a scandal. There is no reason why the World Bank and IMF should think of introducing SAPs to African nations after the World's experience with Germany's SAPs. As to Africans who had said that SAPs are the panacea to African woes, they must be ignorant, wicked or very selfish. The majority of Africans have realized that SAPs are not development programmes. They must be abandoned to restore hope in Africa.

Vision 2010 (1997) is one programme that Nigerians claimed contains the great hope for all Nigerians. What is the basis for the new claim? It is unnecessary that any large space should be devoted to discussing it. It suffice to say that it has the following features. First, its premise remains the HDM. This means that whereas it has wild dreams (non-achievable objectives), it has no growth elements. Second, it re-emphasised the features of the African SAPs – privatization, deregulation (market forces or planlessness) without paying any attention to the primary source of SEGI. A third feature of Vision 2010 is that it contains more sentiments than other Nigeria's planning documents.

The fourth feature of Vision 2010 is that as usual, it was externally motivated like SAPs. Virtually all West African nations had visionary plans at the same time. Just as Nigeria had Vision 2010, so Ghana had Vision 2020 and Gambia Vision 2020. Was this just a coincidence? Africans cannot progress as long as some foreigners do the thinking for them; Vision 2010 has nothing new to offer Nigerians. There is no basis for its implementation. Vision 2010 has no basis for achieving SEGI.

Nigeria's Vision 2010 identified 13 (thirteen) Critical Success Factors (CSF). Employment opportunities were not considered a CSF. The document lamented the existence of unemployment in Nigeria but it did not see it as an issue related to achieving SEGI. This is because Nigeria's planning documents since 1960, including Vision 2010 have never cared about the need to 'think before acting.' Consequently, whereas Vision 2010 pretended to have addressed three important issues: "Where We Are", "Where We Want to Be" and "How To Get There", about Nigeria, it certainly did not address how Nigerians and Nigeria would get to where they want to be by year 2010. As such, Vision 2010 like Nigeria's 5-year plans, 3-year plans and SAPs, can only promote poverty. This is because Vision 2010 like the other planning documents before it does not contain growth elements. No style of implementation will correct the faulty thinking about SEGI underlying Vision 2010. Vision 2010 must be abandoned and forgotten, if Nigerians are to look forward to progress and peace.

In 2003, the Obasanjo administration 1999-2007 merely rename the Nigerian SAPs, NEEDS - National Economic Empowerment and Development Strategy. The claim of emphasis on value reorientation and on fighting corruption in NEEDS were mere sentiments. NEEDS and the proposed NEEDS 2 are premised on the Harrod-Domar Model (HDM). SAPs and NEEDS lack growth-promoting elements. Government having implemented NEEDS during the period 2003-2007, acknowledged that it merely promoted growth without a corresponding increase in employment opportunities - growth without development. Nigeria's plans since independence in 1960 lacked growth-promoting elements. El-Rufai (2007), Honourable Minister, Federal Capital Territory (FCT), 2003-2007, while delivering a keynote address to the National Council on Commerce and Industry at the Musa Yar'Adua Centre, Abuja, observed that with manufacturing contributing less than 4% of the GDP in 2005, Nigeria did not record appreciable level of industrial performance. "Indeed, the trend in the last two decades has been declining performance of the sector and de-industrialisation. Manufacturing as percentage of GDP fell from 8.4% in 1980 to 5.5% in 1999 and 3.8% in 2005." Nigeria adopted SAPs in 1986.

Industrialisation is a learning process: A Theory

Our perception of the development process is that it involves two sets of issues. These are: (i) Fundamentals, or those concerned with technological growth; and (ii) Peripherals, or those concerned with the aftermath or consequences of technological growth – economics, social and political relationships. This perception is represented in figure 6. It explains why those who do not understand the nature of technological growth, the core issues, cannot promote sustainable economic growth.

Technological growth is a learning process. Every man and every woman are born as crying babies. The healthy baby soon begins to babble, that is, learns how to talk, acquires the capabilities to talk and then talks (Ogbimi, 1990). Every other capability including those for producing the modern goods Nigeria and other African nations import is acquired through learning. Western and eastern nations which are described as developed today were technologically backward and were largely agricultural nations for about 2000 years. No one or nation is born with production skills. All types of societies must learn and acquire technological capabilities to be able to solve common problems.

Daniel Lee (1852), wrote that progress implies an advancement from things known to things unknown – an addition to the aggregate wisdom of the world. Hence, except a society makes systematic efforts towards increasing knowledge, progress is impracticable. Schumpeter (1934), wrote that development is internal to a people and a nation. A backward nation waiting and begging foreigners to come and invest in it so that it can achieve SEGI, is only wasting time and other resources and reveling in the bliss of ignorance.

Sustainable Economic Growth, Industrialisation and Development (SEGID) can only be achieved through learning. The value of the learning-man appreciates in a compound fashion with learning intensity and time. Thus, when a person commences an educational or apprenticeship programme, he or she begins from the minimum level in it. Usually, at the end of the first year of learning, the learning-person is promoted to the second level having learnt the things scheduled for the first level. The growth achieved this way is sustainable. At the end of the second year, the learning-person again moves to the third level having completed learning the things in level two. The learning person builds-up capabilities or competence – the ability to do things including dancing, singing, car repair, welding, etc., as he learns. The competence at level three is the cumulative of the competence built-up from levels one, two and three. This build-up of competence continues as long as the learning process continues; the ability to do things increase with build-up of competence. This is how the individual and nation move up the competence-scale. Figure 7 illustrates how the learning process builds-up capabilities, including production strength. This is unlike the case of using a structure like a machine, figure 5. Whereas the production strength of structures like machines decreases with usage and time, the production strength of the learning-man appreciates as he is 'used' in learning and work over time. This explains why the objective value of the experienced engineer and economist are higher than those of the fresh ones. Human experience supports the learning-man theory.

The intrinsic value of the learning-man as a function of learning intensity and time may be represented as (Ogbimi, 1992):

$$M_n = M_0 (1 + r)^n \dots\dots\dots\dots\dots\dots\dots\dots (3)$$

where M_n is the value at time $n = 1, 2, ..n$; M_0 is the initial value before learning commences; and r is the learning rate or intensity. A graphical representation of equation (3) is shown in figure 8. The figure illustrates how learning intensity affects the economic growth of the individual and nation. When more than one person, N, is involved in the learning process, the value function of the contributions of all the-learning-men to the growth of the nation, M_e becomes:

$$M_e = NM_0 (1 + r)^n \dots\dots\dots\dots\dots\dots\dots\dots (4)$$

with notation as in equation (3) maintained.

As many people learn and acquire knowledge and skills in breadth and depth, that is, as N becomes very large, a point is reached when each skill type begins to enjoy the support of all others and an invisible   knowledge and skills-framework is formed (Ogbimi, 1999). The society then achieves industrial maturity (or puberty). The economy becomes diversified, productivity improves dramatically and the society is said to have achieved Industrial Revolution (IR). This transformation may be likened to that which the spider achieves when it transforms many of its single silk-threads into a web. The single thread is a relatively weak structural material which fails under any stress condition. However, the web made from many of the relatively weak silk-threads is a potent tool which catches many small creatures on which the spider feeds.

When a nation achieves the desirable economic transformation, the contribution of the learning-men to the strength of the economy, M'_e becomes(Ogbimi, 1995):

$$M^1_e = NML (1 + r)^n \dots\dots\dots\dots\dots\dots\dots\dots (5)$$

Or more generally,

$$M^{11}_e = 3 \quad 3 \quad 3 \quad 3 \quad 3 \quad N_i M_{oj} L_k (1 + r_l)^n_p \dots.. (6)$$
$$\qquad\qquad i \quad j \quad k \quad l \quad p$$

43

where L represents the transformation and i represents number and types of people in productive activities, j represents the educational/training levels of the workforce, k represents the breadth and depth of linkages among the skill types (strength of theknowledge and skills-framework), r represents rates of learning, while p represents the experiences of the different categories of the workforce.

The industrialization process is illustrated in figure 9. The figure shows how industrialization is achieved. Industrialization is achieved through learning and application of knowledge and skills to solving problems including production. It is a process that matures like the growth of fruits to maturity and ripening. Industrialization is a group effort. Each person in the skill-framework, no matter how versatile, is only a point in a network. He fails readily outside the network. This explains why Nigerians and other Africans perform well abroad where well developed skill-frameworks exist but they do not appear to do well when they return home where a knowledge-and-skills-framework does not exist. This also explains the bad state of Nigeria's erected structures, be they large, medium and or small scale enterprises. In the absence of the desirable knowledge-and-skills framework, individual persons and structures cannot perform well and be sustained in the system.

Relevant Variables for Promoting Industrialization

From equation (6), the relevant variables for measuring sustainable economic growth and for managing an economy are five. The relevant variables are (Ogbimi, 1996a):

(i) N_i, the number of people involved in productive activities or employment level in the nation;

(ii) M_{oj}, the level of education/training of those involved in productive activities;

(iii) L_k, the linkages among the knowledge, skills and sectors in the economy;

(iv) r_i, the learning rate or intensity in the economy, especially that of the workforce; and

44

(v) n_p, the experience of the workforce and the learning history of the society.

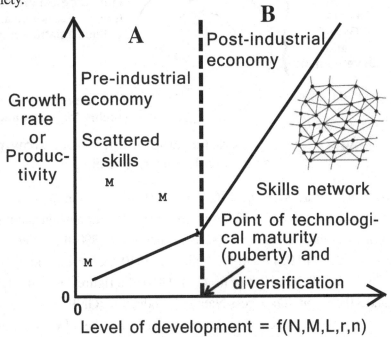

Figure 9 :   The Relationship between the level of development and growth rate.

All of these relevant variables are related to the learning-man and they are directly related to the strength of the economy. This means that the more the number of people involved in productive activities, the higher the average education/training of the workforce, the more the linkages among the knowledge and skills possessed by the workforce and society or by the sectors of the economy, the higher is the learning rate in the society and among the workforce and the more the experience of the society and workforce, the more healthy the economy becomes. These relevant industrialization variables disproved the belief that university education is an elite or privileged endeavour.

The economic progress of the United States was marked by increasing number of workers in manufacturing and construction and increasing average education of

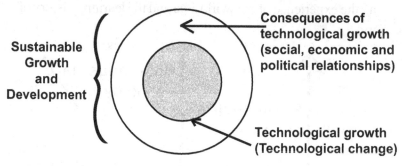

Figure 6: **A model of what sustainable growth and development entail.**

the workforce (Bartlett, *et al.*, 1969). In 1870, the total number of workers, N_i in equation (6) was about 12.9 million, with 6.4 million in agriculture, 2.3 million in manufacture and 750,000 in construction. In 1890, the corresponding figures were 23.7, 10.0, 4.8 and 1.4 million. In 1910, the corresponding figures were 36.7, 11.3, 8.2 and 2.3 million. In 1930, the figures were 47.4, 10.2, 10.8 and 3.0 million. The Gross National Production (GNP) estimates in the period grew in consonance with the increase in the number of workers and the manufacturing strength. Thus in the period 1869 – 1873, the GNP was $9.1 billion, $16.1 billion in the period 1877 – 1881, $24.0 billion during the period 1887 – 1891, $37.1 billion during the period 1897 – 1901, $55.0 billion in the period 1907 – 1911, $73.3 billion in 1920 and $104 billion in 1929. The United States achieved Industrial Revolution during the period 1850 – 1900.

The American economy was $7.63 trillion strong in 1996 (Industry and Environment (2001); the economy was also employing 132.5 million highly knowledgeable and skilled work force in 1998 (U.S. Census Bureau, 2000).

In the 1851 Crystal Palace Industrial Exhibition in London, American goods were the center of attraction. The surprised Britons went to America to find out. They discovered that the strength of American production was in the quality of the workforce. Whereas the functional literacy among the British workforce was about 67 per cent, that among the American workforce was about 90 (ninety) per cent. In the 1980s, America had become the world leader in manufacturing and Japan was in the second position threatening to surpass America in many areas. The worried Americans went to Japan to find out. Again, the Japanese manufacturing strength was in the quality of the workforce. The functional literacy rate among the Japanese workforce was more than 95 (ninety-five) per cent whereas the rate had fallen to 80 per cent, in America (*International Business Week*, 1988).

Empirical evidence quite support our theory that the strength of an economic system is in the workforce. If Nigeria must improve her productivity, it must improve the quality and numerical strength of the workforce. The artisan workforce must be replaced by highly knowledgeable and more skilled workforce.

It is in this sense that the term *human capital* is a misnomer. The learning-man, an appreciating asset (AA) does not need the decoration of capital, a depreciating asset (DA). Gold and diamond as highly prized ornaments do not need the decorations of mud and sand.

Organised intelligence is the new factor of production (Galbraith, 1967). This is an association of men of diverse technical knowledge, experience or other talents, which modern industrial planning requires. It embraces a large number of people and a large variety of talents. It is on the effectiveness of this organization that it is now agreed that the success of modern business enterprises depends. The entrepreneur, individualistic, restless person, with vision, guile and courage was the economist hero long ago, not now (Galbraith, 1967:60).

About 691 million people worked in factories in China in the late 1990s (*Chinese Statistical Bureau*, 1996). But there are less than 40,000 people working in factories in Nigeria (MAN, 1995).

Nigerian factory workers are mainly illiterates; there is probably about one university graduate to about one hundred people among factory workers in Nigeria (Ogbimi

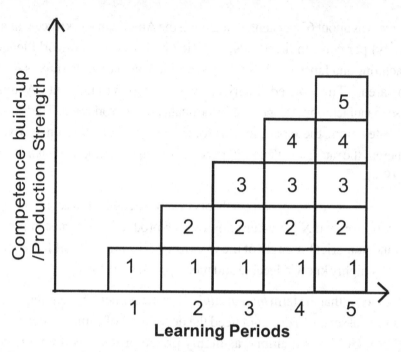

Figure 7 : A Schematic of how competence buids-up in the learning process.

and Akarakiri, 1997). The Nigerian university system has probably not produced one million university graduates since 1914 (NUC, 1995). The National Youth Service Corps (NYSC) Directorate announced in 1998 that one million youths, with National Certificate of Education (NCE), Higher National Diploma (HND) Certificates and University degrees participated in the youth programme during the period 1974-1998. The NYSC commenced in 1974 with NCE, HND and University graduates (*The Guardian*, May 29, 1998, p. 5).

There is about 0.7 graduate, among every 100 people or one graduate to about 140 people in Nigeria. Nigeria's 89 universities now produce about 150,000 university graduates every year. Most of the graduates produced since the early 1980s have not been employed to pursue careers.

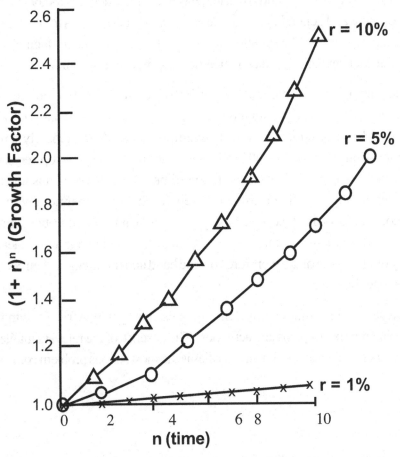

$(1 + r)^n$

n	0	1	2	3	4	5	6	7	8	9	10
r =1	1.00	101	1.02	1.03	1.04	1.05	1.06	1.07	1.08	1.09	1.11
r = 5	1.00	1.05	1.10	1.16	1.22	1.28	1.34	1.41	1.48	1.55	1.63
r=10	1.00	1.10	1.21	1.33	1.46	1.61	1.77	1.95	2.14	2.36	2.59

Figure 8: Graphs of $(1 + r)^n$ vs n from the growth function $P = P_0 (1 + r)^n$, for r = 1, 5 and 10 percent.

There were over 3,300 (three thousand, three hundred) degree-awarding institutions in the united States in the 1985/86 academic year (Johnstone, 1986). More than 22 (twenty-two) per cent of Americans possessed a university degree in 1985/86 academic year. That translated to more than 60 million people with university degrees in America at that time. Over 25 per cent of the population of Western nations (Europe and America) has bachelor's degrees today. This puts the economic and general backwardness of Nigeria and other African nations in a proper perspective. The situation also shows the real challenges facing Nigeria and other African nations today in their development endeavours.

It is pertinent here to note that Vision 2010 Report (1997) urged Nigeria to commercialize education and reduce emphasis on tertiary education. This is probably aimed at reducing graduate unemployment. Unfortunately, a nation without a strong emphasis on all levels of education can only develop very slowly, without achieving industrialization for a long time. The inclusion of this suggestion in the report suggests that those who prepared it were either not aware of or were not mindful of the direct relationship between the number, educational/training level, linkages among the knowledge and skills, the learning rate and the learning history (experience) of the workforce on one hand and the strength of an economy on the other hand.

The presentation in this section demonstrates clearly why Africa is dying with increasing number of plans and activities. The absence of the relevant intellectual framework to guide development activities is the most serious problem confronting all African nations today. It is the same problem for Latin American and Asian nations.

Western intelligentsia have been brought up to believe that capital investment is the primary source of sustainable economic growth and industrialization (SEGI). Westerners have indoctrinated 'learned' Africans, Latin Americans and Asians, to believe same. Consequently, all we have been witnesses to are: World Bank and IMF urging African and Latin American nations to secure loans and provide favourable environment for inflow of capital from the West, so that African nations can erect complex structures and achieve effortless development. UNIDO and African and Latin American experts agree with the Brentton Woods institutions' view about development. This has been the situation for decades. This is how the United Nations special agencies and Western intelligentsia have misled and ruined many developing nations, especially African nations for many decades.

Efforts of the Brentton Woods institutions and Western experts and their *students* in the developing world have all been distractions preventing developing nations from focusing attention on learning and the relevant variables for promoting industrialisation. African, Latin American and some Asian nations have therefore been 'planting cooked seeds' and experiencing decay and retrogression. The sad situation has now been revealed, it has to change.

4

THE WEALTH CREATING CYCLE (WCC)

The wealth creation process is a dynamic and non-equilibrium one in which increased value and utility are created. It has been observed (Ogbimi, 1992) that three non-exclusive economic groups characterize a wealth creating-economy. These are:

(i)   the investing public and government;
(ii)   the educational/learning institutions; and
(iii)   the production and service units.

Their interrelationships are as shown in figure 10. This has been identified as the Wealth Creating Cycle - the WCC (Ogbimi, 1997a).

The public and government make input of depreciating assets (DAs) like money, other materials, time, etc., into learning institutions, through the linkage one (L-1). The learning institutions convert the DAs into appreciating assets (AAs) – the learning-man and learning woman and their knowledge and skills. The conversion of DAs into AAs is the critical phase in the wealth creating process; wealth cannot be created in the absence of this critical conversion. Learning institutions input the learning-people and their knowledge and skills through linkage two (L-2) into the production system. The production and service units use the new knowledge and skills to create wealth (increased value and utility).

The learning-people and their knowledge create wealth through the following and other steps (Ogbimi, 1998a):

1.   Repeated use of knowledge and skills,
2.   Multiplication of knowledge and skills as in teaching, and
3.   Increasing value of the learning-man as he is 'used' in learning

and production because he acquires increased creative ability as he is used.

The production and service units pass the wealth to the public and pay increased taxes to government through linkage three (L-3). The value/utility of the materials including money and time input into L-1 is less than the output through L-3. This

52

is the consequence of the wealth created in the cycle, the WCC. This means that, to create wealth in a nation, government and the investing public (group 1), educational/learning institutions (group 2) and production and service units (group 3) play unique roles. Government and the investing public cannot play the role of the learning institutions. Similarly, production units cannot play the role of learning institutions and vice versa.

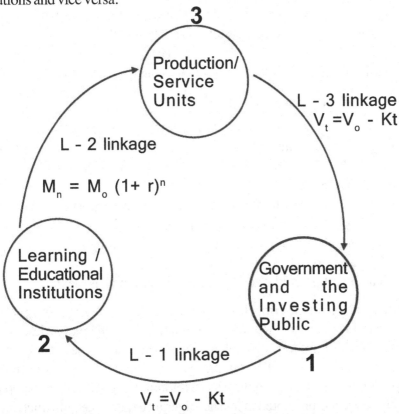

Figure 10: The relationships among the main economic groups in an economy, the Wealth Creating Cycle (WCC).

This shows that the concept of private sector-led industrialisation derives from faulty thinking. The private sector by its individualistic nature does not promote common good, it only promotes wealth concentration in a nation. Again, Russell (1967), observed that individualism discourages the development of scientific capabilities because developing them demands cooperation among many people and a close-knit society.

Organized intelligence is the new factor of production which modern industrial technology planning requires. The industrial system must rely on external sources for the supply of talent. Unlike capital, it is not within the industrial system; it is not something that the firm can supply itself. The mere possession of capital is no guarantee that the required talent can be obtained and organized (Galbraith, 1967).

The Poverty Promoting Cycle (PPC)

Mankind has knowingly or inadvertently preferred to operate in the poverty promoting cycle (PPC) through the neglect of L-1 and L-2 and the creation of a new linkage, (L-1-3) (Ogbimi, 1997a). Figure 11 shows the WCC and PPC in perspective. The cycle made up of:
1.   The Investing Public and Government (group 1) through,
2.   Linkage one – three (L-1-3), through,
3.   The Production and Service Units (group 3) through,
4.   Linkage three (L-3), and back to,
5.   The Investing Public and Government (group 1), is the PPC.

The PPC is devoid of the critical conversion of DAs into AAs by group 2 which is indispensable to wealth creation. The equation on each linkage describes the type of resources that flow through it. Nigeria has indeed been trapped in the PPC, since 1960. The emphasis in the cycle is immaterial, be it the small and medium enterprises (SMEs), industrial development, agricultural development, etc., only poverty is promoted in it. The Nigerian experience quite matches this analysis. This explains why poverty is increasing in Nigeria. Nigerians would be poorer with time as long as the nation remains trapped in the PPC.

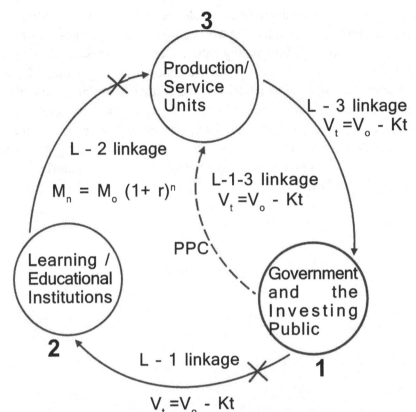

Figure 11 : *The main economic groups and their relationships to poverty promotion and wealth creation in an economy.*

The distinction betweeen a business company or a firm and a nation is quite important. A nation must achieve sustainable economic growth and ultimately achieve industrialisation to increase its wealth and the living standard of the citizens. A nation must educate and train its citizens perpetually to grow. Nations do not just place advertisement to assemble the people to work in the millions of types of positions needed in a typical modern economy. Thus, Nigeria cannot hire people from all other nations and expect to assemble them in Nigeria to enable Nigeria achieve the modern IR. But a company can assemble people from Britain, America and Japan, and a few factory-hands in Nigeria, and operate profitably as a business organisation. While the primary objective of a business company is to make profit or income which is generally defined as sales or total revenue minus total cost, a nation measures improvement in the welfare of citizens. A business organissation can operate profitably in a stagnating nation. Hence, business organisations can operate profitably and maximize profit in a nation operating in the PPC. Selfish government officials may own business and claim that governance is all about providing the conducive environment for business organisations to operate profitably. A good government is one that caters for all groups. A good government ensures that it operates in the WCC by supporting education, training graduates of educational institutions to acquire complementary practical skills and by promoting full employment policy.

5

FRUITS OF INDUSTRIALSIATION

The Manufacturers Association of Nigeria (MAN) in its book, *Nigerian Industrial Directory* (1987), listed ten sectors to which its members belong. These were: (i) Food, Beverages and Tobacco; (ii) Chemicals and Pharmaceuticals; (iii) Domestic and Industrial Plastics and Rubber; (iv) Basic Metal, Iron and Steel and Fabricated Metal Products; (v) Pulp, Paper and Paper Products, Printing and Publishing; (vi) Electrical and Electronics; (vii) Textile, Wearing Apparel and Leather; (viii) Wood and Wood products including Furniture; (ix) Non-Metal Mineral Products; and (x) Motor Vehicle and Miscellaneous Assembly. These sectors only exist in name, but not in terms of production activities. Similarly, sectors such as maritime, aviation, tourism, transportation, etc., only exist in nominal terms. Mere erection of airports and hiring of aircrafts do not create an aviation sector. Also, building of ports and hiring of ocean liners do not create a maritime industry.

The Nigerian economy according to UNIDO (1988) is a dual one. It is made up of the indigenous group and the parasitic Organized Private Sector (OPS). Indeed, it is a tripartite economy with the indigenous artisan/craft production system as one part, the OPS as the second part while the oil and gas industry constitute the third part. There are virtually no activity-linkages among the three parts. This is one reason the economy is very weak in terms of production or in solving any particular problem.

The flourishing of the various sectors of an economy as it is the case in modern economies, comes with industrialization (industrial maturity). Western and eastern economies many centuries ago were monosectoral – they only had agriculture as their main activity. Every other thing they did, cloth weaving for example, was closely related to their main activity – agriculture. The various sectors only began to flourish with the achievement of industrialisation. Diversification is achieved after industrialization. Diversification of an economy is an organic process; it is not a mechanical process achieved by investing in the agricultural and communication sectors.

Transforming native agriculture into modern one is a fruit of the industrialisation process; no amount of domestic and foreign investments per se, can transform native agriculture into modern agriculture (Ogbimi, 1994b). The Americans tried mass importation as a strategy for development but quickly realized that it was a futile effort (Moore, 1801).

The state of the construction, transportation, communication, manufacturing, health, agricultural and educational sectors and the ability to sustain good infrastructure depend on the state of industrialisation in a society. High performance in the various sectors of an economy, diversification, comes as the fruit of industrialisation. This is because it is the inputs from industry that go to improve productivity in agriculture and others. No amount of capital investment per se, can sustain good infrastructural network in an agrarian economy.

The lesson from this is that it is not enough to claim that there are many sectors in an economy making demand on scarce resources. The concept of opportunity cost is a well known one – it is what one forgoes for any particular choice of action. If a pupil has to decide between watching a video tape and going to a coaching class, and he decides to go to the coaching class, watching the video tape is the foregone opportunity or the opportunity cost. Our analysis shows, that the performance of all sectors depends on the state of industrialisation of the economy. We also know now that industrialisation is promoted through learning and acquiring knowledge, skills and capabilities and applying these in solving problems, including those associated with production. It is therefore education and industrialisation that a young nation should emphasize first to promote common well-being. Nigeria should as such begin to emphasize learning activities to promote industrialisation. Doing anything else or spreading too thin or merely erecting structures is tantamount to displaying stupidity. Only one thing is needed: educate and train the people (develop the people) so that the people can build the needed roads and telecommunication networks and other structures. To erect complex structures without developing the people is to act stupidly like the father who neglects the education and training of his children and focuses on building houses for them to inherit.

6

THEORY OF LEARNING, EMPLOYMENT, AUTOMATION, PRODUCTIVITY AND INFLATION

Ogbimi (1990a), observed that every production process or system has an intrinsic value, V_p. This value has two aspects to it. These are the value of the goods/services obtainable from the system, V_g and the value of the learning opportunities associated with the system, V_1. This relationship may be represented as:

$$V_p = V_g + V_1 \quad \text{..} (7)$$

The automobile repair workshop for example, provides the service of car repairs and also has learning opportunities for training apprentices. A typical industrial plant produces industrial products and also has learning opportunities. Similarly, any economy produces goods and provides services and also has learning opportunities.

A nation may decide to neglect the learning opportunities in the economy and concentrate on the production of goods/services. Unfortunately, learning is the source of new knowledge and skills and improved productivity. Any nation that neglects learning, risks stagnation.

In a progressive society, V_p grows from increases in both V_g and V_1, because as learning takes place, improved knowledge and skills are acquired and input into the system. These (the improved knowledge and skills) are the fundamental bases for improving productivity and total production. Primitive nations which neglect the learning opportunities in their production systems cannot establish the necessary production linkages demanded by a modern economy. They also cannot bridge the gap between theoretical and practical skills; and they cannot achieve rapid industrialisation. Nations which neglect the learning opportunities in their economies experience mass unemployment, courtesy of the neglect of the opportunities for expanding the production base of the economy. Societies which neglect the learning opportunities in their economies cannot experience innovations because learning and acquiring new knowledge and skills and applying these in production are the bases for achieving innovations.

Equation (7) illustrates that the real value of the interactions among nations is in learning and acquiring new knowledge and skills. It is when the people in a production system learn and understand the problems in it that they are able to solve them and improve productivity. In the absence of learning and acquisition of new knowledge, productivity stagnates or drops.

It is the learning component of the value of a production system that matters in the interaction among nations. The lessons of history show that one society learns from another and this provides the basis for improving the productivity of the society with the lower productivity. No society has achieved modern industrialiSation in isolation (Ogbimi, 1988). Europe began the modern era with almost total dependence on the Chinese, Indian and Islamic cultures – the Great Medieval Civilizations (Cardwell, 1974). Indeed, England was accused by continental Europe of copying its inventions and being unoriginal, just before England achieved the first modern industrial revolution. The learning society is the progressive one. Americans later learnt from Europeans, and Japanese learnt from Europeans and Americans. It is probably the turn of Africans to learn from the rest of the world – Europeans, Americans and Asians in the sequence of one nation learning from the other. This is the real benefit of foreign investment in modern time. The real value of foreign investment therefore, lies in the opportunities they provide for learning about the production/service systems in other societies.

The real value of foreign investment does not lie in the glamour of board membership, market, equity shares and dividends, or in the menial jobs they provide for illiterates in a developing nation. Unfortunately, Nigerian economic planners have not realized this and they have had no reason for stressing the real value of foreign investments.

The ability to learn from a productive system depends on the extent the person concerned understands the principles underlying the production. Illiterates cannot learn from a sophisticated production system. As people learn and understand the production activities in the various sectors of an economy, the relevant linkages become established.

Equation (7) was further analysed by Ogbimi (1995). The method of analysis was as shown in figure 12. With true inflation (I) defined as the ratio, P/V, where "P" is the seller's price and "V" is the producer's cost, it was demonstrated that the productivity and inflation curves are the images of each other. The uppe curve (the parabola) was identified as the inflation parabola while the lower curve (the hyperbola) was identified as the productivity (or production) hyperbola. In other words, improved productivity is the true antidote (remedy) for inflation. Numerically, this is expressed as:

$$-dV/V = dI/I \ldots\ldots\ldots\ldots\ldots\ldots\ldots\ldots\ldots\ldots\ldots\ldots\ldots\ldots (8)$$

Figure 13 shows the relationships among the level of employment; learning, knowledge and skills; and the relevant automation in a production system; and the level of productivity and the level of inflation in an economy. The results show that any economy may be characterized by one of three fundamental stati. These are co-existent: (I) Low Productivity, High Unemployment and High Inflation (Stagflation); (II) Optimum Productivity, High Employment (low unemployment) and Minimal Inflation; and (III) Low Productivity, Full Employment and High Inflation.

Developing nations are in position (I); they are confronted by low productivity, mass unemployment (low employment) and high inflation problems. England and other western nations faced these problems for many centuries. When western nations achieved industrialization (industrial transformation), they became closer to position (II) and were able to solve the problems and experienced high productivity (optimum productivity), high employment (low unemployment) and minimal inflation. Industrialized nations are closer to position II. Position (III) is a

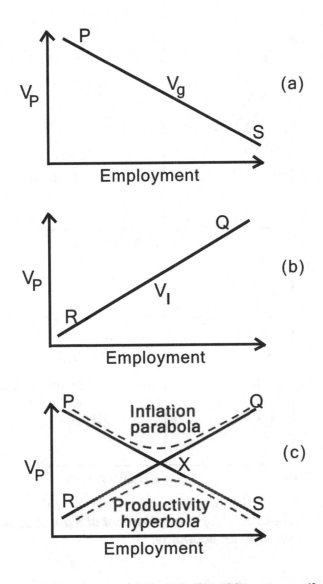

Figure 12 :- Illustration of the ralationships among the values obtainable from a production process, V_p, the value of goods / services obtainable from it, V_g, and the value of the learning opportunities associated with the process, V_r

63

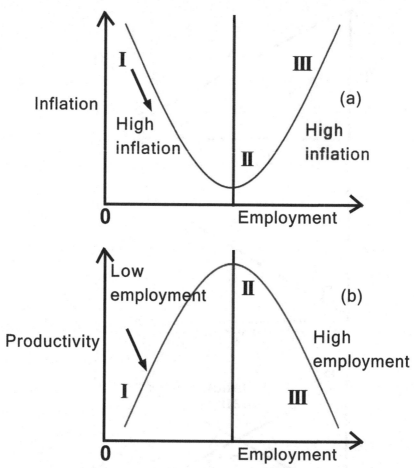

Figure 13 :-The Relationships of Inflation (a) and Productivity (b) to employment of a productive labour in an economy.

theoretical one, because no nation employs citizens to that level. It is however, an important fanalytical fact to note.

Western intelligentsia, especially Phillips (1958) and the World Bank and IMF workers have been confusing position (I) with position (III). However, our analysis, figure 13 makes it easy to distinguish between the positions. In position

(III), there is a trade-off relationship between unemployment and inflation; reduction of unemployment (increase in employment) increases inflation, and vice versa. Whereas in position (I), reduction of unemployment (increase in employment) improves productivity and reduces inflation. The application of Phillips' curve trade-off relationship between inflation and unemployment assumes that the nation is in position (III). All developing nations are in position (I) and not position (III). The World Bank and IMF have always been applying Phillips' curve in African and Latin American nations in error. This has been a grievous error and it is one other way the Brentton Woods institutions have mismanaged developing nations for many decades.

The management of an economy from one status to another, say from position (I) to position (II), or position (II) to position (III), is a fundamental change – a transformation, one which demands a quantum input of quality knowledge and skills into the production system or economy. Industrialization moves an economy from position (I) towards position (II).

The theory of employment, productivity and inflation, again, shows that learning is the fundamental basis of growth and development. The theory also demonstrates that the characteristics of man's production aids – machines, are dependent on the knowledge man possesses for making them. Man makes tools and machinery to help him in doing certain things, but not learning. This is because man uniquely learns, machines do not learn. This is why machines cannot supplant man in the production process. When machines supplant man, growth and development in that society will stop.

Man did not make the internal combustion engine in the Stone Age (pre-3000 B.C.), probably because he did not have the knowledge to do so. Learning in production improves productivity because it enables man to acquire practical skills and discover the best process in production. As man learns and acquires knowledge and skills in breadth and depth, his production aids become more sophisticated and efficient. The state of an economy, as such, depends strongly on the level of

65

employment (the quality and quantity of knowledge and skills being applied in production) in it.

Industrialisation is a Transformational Change

Our analysis suggests that Nigeria and other developing nations are in status (I). The solution to Nigeria's co-existent problems of mass unemployment, low productivity and high inflation, as such, is the introduction of large quantities of high quality knowledge and skills into production activities in the economy (increase in employment). How can this be done? Interestingly, history and logic show that learning, sustainable growth, industrialisation and development are not equilibrium processes dependent on the supply and demand of labour. Rather, they are transformational (or non-equilibrium) changes, solely dependent on the learning intensity and the rate at which new knowledge and skills flow into production activities in a society. This may be represented as in figure 14 (Ogbimi, 1995).

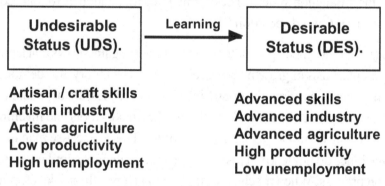

Figure 14 :- The transformation which characterizes Industrialization

It is a fundamental learning intensity-dependent change from an undesirable status (UDS) to a desirable status (DES). While the UDS is characterized by artisan/craft skills, artisan industry and agriculture, low productivity and high unemployment, the DES is characterized by advanced skills, advanced industry and agriculture, high productivity and low unemployment.

The British, American, French and German economies have been transformed for centuries without reverting back to the artisan/craft economies they were for

66

a long time before their transformation. This is a proof that industrialisation is a transformation and not an equilibrium or supply-demand relationship. Examples of other transformational changes are the growth of a baby into adulthood, the inflation of a football or car tyre and the filling of a tank with water. We inflate our tyres to a desirable pressure, say 32 atmospheres; we do not wait for the atmosphere to inflate tyre for us. We also force water into a water tank; we do not wait for nature to get water into the tank. The adult man never reverts to a baby again. It is in this sense that educational/learning institutions can be called "economic pumps." They are economic pumps because we can use the knowledge generated in them to transform an artisan-economy like Nigeria's into an industrialised one rapidly, just as a mechanical pump can be used to inflate a good tyre rapidly.

An economy may therefore be likened to a football; they both bounce. Whereas the content of the bouncing ball is high-pressured air or gas, the content of the bouncing economy is a well educated/trained workforce armed with its high quality knowledge and skills. The weak economy in this context is one devoid of a well educated/trained workforce.

The foregoing warns us that foreign investments, hiring of expatriates and importation of complex structures are not the solutions to the problems of mass unemployment, lack of industrialisation and low productivity in Nigeria. How soon Nigeria becomes industrialised depends on how hard Nigerians work toward acquiring the relevant knowledge and skills. This means that the sooner Nigerians acquire adequate knowledge, skills and capabilities and apply these in solving problems including production, the sooner will Nigeria achieve modern industrial transformation.

In the context of our model, an economy may be inflated like a football with a 'pump' or be left to the atmosphere (allow market forces and deregulation) to inflate. Western and Eastern nations largely waited for market forces to plan for them; they achieved evolutionary industrialisation through laissez-faire learning over about 2000 years. Nigeria must learn from the experiences of older nations. Nigeria must plan to achieve rapid industrialisation through intensive learning and acquisition of knowledge and skills and applying these in production.

The Advantages the Imitator Enjoys

It is the foolish person who visits his friend and when he eats a delicious meal there, he would ask: when will you prepare this type of meal again so that I can come and eat again. The wise person would ask: this meal is tasty, how do you prepare it, what are the ingredients? This is probably the basis of the Chinese adage which says: 'teach me how to fish so that I can catch fish myself whenever I want to eat fish.' The Asians intuitively know that self-reliance comes form learning and not from begging. The Nigeria economy may be likened to a very sick patient, too sick to eat, who must be fed intravenously. The medical doctors feed the very sick patient intravenously in attempt to save his life. The Nigerian economy may also be likened to an anaemic patient who must be supplied blood (critical requirement) speedily through blood transfusion. Knowledge and skills and human activities constitute the "blood" of an economy. Our understanding that achieving sustainable economic growth and industrialisation is a transformation and not an equilibrium change, enables us to know that the learning channels in the economy can be used to increase the knowledge and skills and human production activities in the economy and restore life to it speedily. This is what we must plan to achieve speedily in Nigeria. It is unfortunate that Africans are ignorantly talking of market forces or planlessness as a preferred development strategy for Africa in today's world where innovations are being orchestrated through planning in the other blocks of the world.

Nigeria and other African nations like the foolish individual has been spending very large amounts of money importing modern products from Europe, America and Asia for decades, without thinking seriously of how to produce them. Nigeria has been spending about 40 per cent of her annual importation bill on machinery and transport equipment (Ogbimi, 1994a). This is how Nigeria has been planning to transform her economy. There is a natural lesson that warns Nigeria of the futility of her approach to effecting the modernization of her economy.

Learned Nigerians claim that Nigeria does not have to re-invent the wheel. However, in any particular household, where more than one child is born, each child spends a characteristic time learning how to talk before talking. That is, the "talking times" of the children in a household vary depending on their positions in the household and other factors. Figure 15 illustrates our observation about the relationship between the talking times (T_t) of children in households and their position at birth (Ogbimi, 1990).

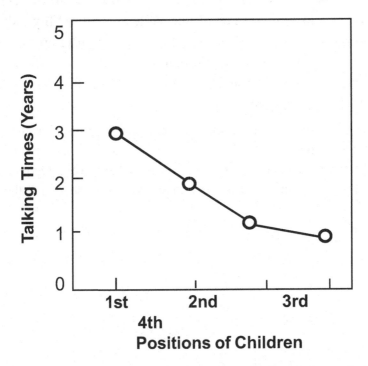

Figure 15 :- The Talking Times of the children in households: Pioneers spend longer times, followers save time in learning how to talk.

The first child in the new household takes the longest time to talk because he has the least interactions with people in the house (lowest learning intensity) among the children. The mother and father working hard to set the new household on a solid foundation cannot have much time for the first born. The second child has the first child to interact with in addition to the parents (higher learning intensity) and takes a shorter time to learn how to talk. Subsequent children take shorter times till the time remains about constant. The advantages the imitator has is that he can learn at higher intensity and progress speedier than his pioneer brother who learnt slowly because he had no one to learn from; he can learn faster and save time. It is not true that the second child need not learn how to talk because the first child had already learnt how to do so. The child who has learning disability and fails to babble grows up to be a dumb. Indeed, the talented pianist must learn the ordinary tunes before using his talents to compose extra-ordinary tunes. Learning always precedes perfection or expertise. How soon the learner becomes an expert depends on his learning intensity.

The progressive society is one that combines learning and consumption; the imitator is a hybridizer. Hence the technological development process may also be described as a hybridizing process or a mixing or blending process (Ogbimi, 1998); the more the knowledge involved in the blending process, the stronger is the hybrid produced.

7

THE NATURE OF THE SKILL-ACQUISITION PROCESS

It has been noted that all capabilities, including those for talking and the production of the modern goods Nigeria and other African nations import every year, are not innate to any individual or race; they are acquired through learning. But Nigerians have been learning for a long time. Nigeria has an expanded educational system. Why have Nigerians not developed the relevant skills for producing Nigeria's needs?

Nigeria has Mediocre Workforce

European Universities existed for over 600 years before the European Industrial Revolution (IR). Oxford was established in the eleventh century (Davies, 1969), while Bologna and Salerno in Italy were established in the thirteenth century (Wiet *et al.*, 1975). It is therefore not the establishment of educational systems *per se*, that determines how soon a society achieves industrialisation, but the purpose for which they were built and how a society ensures that the systems play their special roles in the nation's industrialisation endeavour. Pre-World Wars European universities were established as private institutions.

Historically, educational systems exist for a long time before playing an active role in the industrialisation process. This is because of the nature of the skill-acquisition process and the industrialisation process itself.

Two types of skills may be acquired. These are theoretical skills (TSs) and practical skills (PSs); anyone who acquires either type alone, is a mediocre (Ogbimi, 1991). In both the now developed and developing nations, formal education produces theoreticians (mediocres). The informal sector's apprenticeship system also produces those with limited practical skills, artisans, mediocres too.

Thus, Nigeria has mediocre-workforce because it produces mediocres from its formal and informal manpower-developing sources. Both formal and informal manpower development efforts in Nigeria do not go through the complete cycle that equips people with both theoretical and practical skills. The secondary school graduate acquires theoretical knowledge alone, he is a mediocre. The polytechnic graduate is very poorly equipped in terms of both theoretical and practical skills. The university graduate is well equipped in terms of theoretical knowledge (principles) alone.The artisan lack theoretical knowledge but possess limited practical skills.

The Industrial Training Fund (ITF) and the National Directorate of Employment (NDE) schemes are haphazard programmes which do nothing tangible to address the problems of lack of relevant productical skill (PRSs), low productivity, lack of industrialization and mass unemployment. ITF and NDE did not originate from a clear understanding of the skill acquisition process. Both the ITF and NDE schemes give too little training to poorly prepared people. NDE especially emphasizes individualism rather than the group effort that industrialization demands. The less known training scheme for engineering graduates, the Supervised Industrial Training Scheme for Engineers (SITSE) planned by the Council of Registered Engineers of Nigeria (COREN) (see *Daily Times*, Monday, April 15, 1991), also did not originate from a clear understanding of the knowledge and skills acquisition process, and does not address the problem of lack of relevant production knowledge and skills in Nigeria.

This is why they are not making the expected impact. Industrialisation is a scientific process. The Western Industrial Revolution was characterized by 8 (eight) innovations by 1800 A.D. (Amrine, et al., 1982). Six of them (75 per cent) were conceived and developed in England and one (12.5 per cent) each was developed in America and France. The IR probably took place in England first because England was the first nation to be ready for it scientifically. The lesson here is that an illiterate and superstitutious society cannot achieve Industrial Revolution.

Correspondence Among Science, Specialization and Productivity

Science is the knowledge of nature. Technology is the application of the knowledge of nature to solving the problems confronting mankind. Science is to technology what vocabulary and syntax are to a language. Science as such, is the building block of technology. Any society planning technological development must first plan for the development of a corresponding scientific base. No nation develops high technological capabilities without first developing the necessary scientific capabilities.

Experience teaches us that there are usually many more blocks than rooms and buildings in the art of building houses. Thus, the scientific population of a society must be much larger than the technological population. The normal and abnormal relationships between the scientific and technological populations in a society are represented in Figure 16. The normal relation cannot be achieved quickly in a market economy (an economy in which market forces or planlessness or profit motives alone determine course of action). Nigeria cannot achieve rapid industrialization with the existing market-determined choice of programmes and enrolment in universities and other tertiary institutions. Profit motives alone cause economic distortions which in turn cause unemployment and reduce the effective production capacity of an economic system (Ogbimi, 1994a). Technological development must be planned; it must not be left to market forces, if it is to be rapid.

Adam Smith (1776), observed that specialization improves productivity significantly. He first pointed out the advantages of division of labour (specialization) in a practical situation. He noticed that pin-making involved eighteen steps and that in the absence of division of labour and one man has to perform all the functions, he can only produce 20 pins a day. But when 10 (ten) men were employed, they produced 48,000 (forty-eight thousand) pins, an average of 4,800 pins per person per day. Specialization in this case improved productivity 240 (two hundred and forty) times.

To achieve rapid industrialization in Nigeria, there is need for specialization in developing the Relevant Production Skills (RPSs) for solving the problems confronting Nigeria. Educational systems should be seen as institutions specialized

73

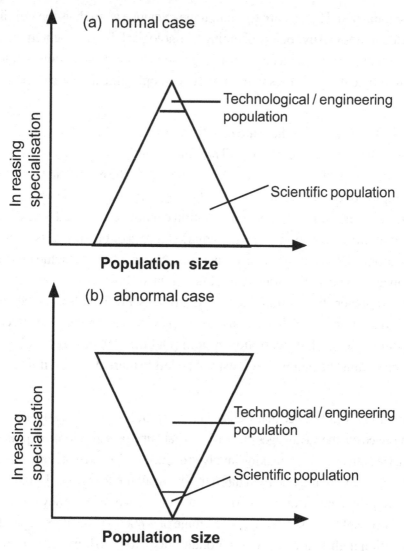

Figure 16 :- *The relationships between scientific and technological / engineering population in a society : (a) shows a nor-*
mal *relationship with the scientific population*
much larger *than the technolofical / engineering*
pupulation;

(b) is the abnormal case with everyone trying to be a specialist.

in equipping the youths with sound principles (theoretical skills). Practical skills must be acquired in the less restrictive production settings outside educational institutions. This is because practical skills are largely acquired in a working situation (Bright and van Lamsweerde, 1993). This is how Nigeria can take advantage of the special positive impact of specialization in accelerating her industrialisation process and improving her productivity correspondingly.

Climbing the Technological Ladder

Technological development may be likened to a ladder-climbing process; it is not a haphazard process but a step-wise one (Ogbimi, 1990). Learning progresses from the learner's position to the experts position (Stahl, 1990). Learning results in relatively permanent changes in knowledge, skills and other behaviours (Klausmeier, 1985).

Nigeria needs to climb the technological ladder rapidly to achieve a speedy industrialization. Progress in the industrialisation process demands higher quality workforce and greater application of more advanced knowledge and skills to solving problems than obtains in an artisan economy.

There is therefore a correspondence between the quality of workforce on the one hand and the productivity and quality of production of the workforce on the other hand. The different global communities have achieved different production stages at different times. History has records of organized (artisan/craft), mechanized, engineered/automated and cybernated production systems (Becker, 1983). Figure 17 shows the probable correspondence between educational qualifications of the workforce of a society and the production type.

In societies where the workforce is made up of mainly illiterates, primary and secondary school leavers or artisans/craftsmen, the production is characterized by crude tools like cutlass, hoe and axe and muscular exertion. The corresponding production and productivity are very low and so is the quality. Mechanised, engineered, automated and cybernated production systems demand sophisticated workforce like a few secondary school graduates, many university graduates

Production systems Educational systems

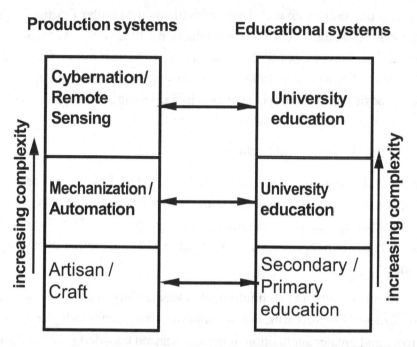

**Figure 17 :- Schematic of the correspondence between production
and educational systems : the substantive education
of   the workforce determines the sophistry of the
production   system.**

and those with higher degrees. Progressing from one production level to a more sophisticated one entails the application of more theoretical science in production. The Nigerian situation is the artisan/craft type characterized by crude tools. This is why the productivity is low.

Nigeria must climb to a higher level of the technology ladder to improve productivity, achieve industrialisation and solve unemployment problem. To do this, she has to create an industrialisation vanguard.

Climbing the technological ladder rapidly demands that there be a rapid development of many people who possess both theoretical and practical skills to advanced levels. These are also to face challenges frequently, so that they can develop the relevant production skills (RPSs) for solving the common problems confronting their society and stimulate rapid industrialisation. This is the set of people that may be called the industrialisation vanguards (IVs). Nigeria does not have IVs today. But Nigeria must create them to initiate a rapid industrialization process.

A mediocre workforce (one with either theoretical knowledge alone or practical skills alone) or an illiterate workforce, cannot ascend the ladder; it is not equipped to do so. Figure 18 illustrates the relationship among theoretical skills (TSs), practical skills (PSs) and relevant production skills (RPSs) (Ogbimi, 1998). The RPSs is the limiting one. While individuals may learn and acquire TSs and PSs, RPSs are developed as individuals and nations face challenges in the working place. For example, the electric motor may be used to make a grinder, an engine for a boat and as a component of an air-conditioner or a refrigerator. The specific skills needed to adapt the electric motor to different uses are the RPSs for the challenges posed by the specific needs. If a society has not developed the RPSs for the fishing industry it is not likely to be able to adapt the motor to help the petty fisherman in it.

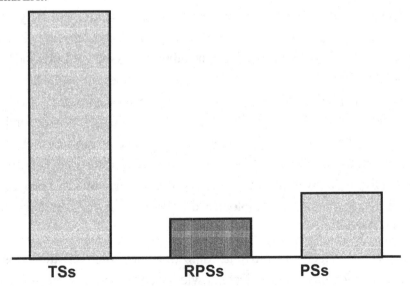

Figure 18 :- The relative magnitude among Theoretical Skills (TSs), Practical Skills (PSs) and the Relevant Production Skills (RPSs); RPSs are the limiting skills.

The skill-acquisition process may also be likened to that in which the components of a balanced food-basket are assembled. Just as the assembler moves from one point to the other in a market or grocery, buying one item at a time, so the skill-acquiring person ought to move from one knowledge/skill-acquiring position to another, acquiring knowledge and skills and relevant production skill till he becomes versatile and confident, and highly employable. Acquiring TSs, PSs and RPSs may be likened to climbing a series of well-separated trees, one after the other. In climbing any of the trees, the climber begins from the foot. Similarly, to develop the RPSs for a society, the skill-acquiring individuals must begin from the lowest level of theoretical and practical skills, if the learning-man is to acquire capabilities effectively. He must not leap-frog or jump steps, but he can learn rapidly and save time.

The technology ladder is therefore rather an unusual one to climb. Its possible form judging from our understanding of the nature of technology and the skill-acquisition process is as shown in figure 19. A society does not begin to climb the technology ladder till the people have completely understood the principles and practices associated with the existing technologies. It is only the society that uses its consumption opportunities to learn intensively that can become the hybridization (blending) box for its own technology and others, to produce hybrids and become a leader (Ogbimi, 1998). It is only after a nation has understood the fundamental theories (step 1) and practices (step 2) of existing technologies, that it can begin to think independently. It is impossible for the people of a society to depend on the thoughts of other nationals and progress rapidly. Once a people has achieved the independent thinking status (ITS), progress comes speedily because the other steps leading to innovations follow readily. The ladder shows that copying (step 6), is an advanced stage of technological development. Nigeria and Nigerians are not yet ready for it.

The obstacle to Nigeria's rapid industrialization therefore is creating those who possess both advanced theoretical knowledge and practical skills – those who understand the principles and practices of the technologies Nigeria consumes today. The Nigerian university graduate equipped with advanced theory is a mediocre.

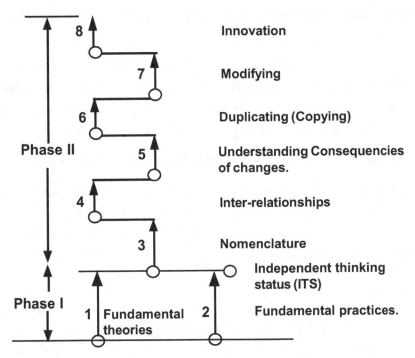

Figure 19 :- Schematic of the Technology Development Ladder.

Can he be made the vanguard? The Nigerian artisan is also a mediocre, with little practical skills. Can the artisan be made the Nigerian industrialization vanguard?

In the analysis entitled, "Innovative Maintenance as a Prerequisite for Industrialization in Third World Nations (Ogbimi, 1991)," transforming the university graduate especially the scientist and engineer into the industrialization vanguards was the choice. The reason advanced was that university graduates already possess the necessary theoretical knowledge, they only need to acquire the complementary practical skills. The artisan could not be the immediate choice, because he possesses only minimal practical skills. He would need more than ten years to complete primary, secondary and tertiary education programmes to acquire the necessary theoretical knowledge and practical skills for independent thinking.

However, it must be added that a team-vanguard made up of the artisan/craftsman and university graduate scientist and engineer would be the ideal thing for Nigeria today. Nigeria needs a combination of all men and women with some skills but the university graduate scientist and engineer would have to lead the team.

Specific Sources for Practical Skills for Scientists and Engineers

Where would the university scientist and engineer acquire the complementary practical skills that would make them think independent of books and become the Nigerian industrialisation vanguards? Should Nigeria expand the teaching facilities in universities (laboratories) and ensure that the students acquire them before leaving universities? No.

This is for two main reasons. First, specialization – universities should specialize in equipping students with principles. They should organize laboratories to illustrate principles, not production. Second, the working place and its unlimited challenges are the sources of practical skills. Laboratories and university campuses can only provide limited opportunities for acquiring practical skills.

Hence the rest of the economy, especially the production sector should serve as the source of complementary practical skills for the products of educational systems. It is in the economy that opportunities for acquiring practical experiences abound, not in university laboratories. The importance of specialization has been demonstrated in discussing the process of wealth creation and the roles of specific groups in the economy in chapter 4.

Thus for Nigeria to initiate a rapid industrialization process, it is the university graduate who is to be transformed into the industrialisation vanguard to lead the desired transformation. The university graduate is to use the learning opportunities in the economy – artisan workshops, factory floor work settings, farms and other places, where opportunities for practical skills abound to acquire complementary practical skills.

It is the university graduate, especially the scientist and engineer who should adopt the innovative maintenance approach to acquiring practical skills with respect to the technologies consumed in Nigeria, today, to complement the theoretical skills he acquires in the university. Innovative maintenance entails the following thoughts and activities (Ogbimi, 1991a):

(i)   Mastering the normal functioning and inter-relationships among the parts and subsystems of all machinery and equipment in use.

(ii)   Studying the trends in equipment imported from one source and among equipment from different sources.

(iii)   Studying the residual faults or limitations that are invariably present in equipment and

(iv)   Analysing the information gathered from maintenance and repair operations and from interactions with users and suppliers of equipment and machinery.

Any set of people that is able to do the foregoing with respect to the technologies consumed in Nigeria would serve as the industrialization vanguard for the Nigerian industrialisation endeavour. One expects the engineering and science university graduates to carry out the foregoing innovative maintenance thoughts and activities in such learning places as:

-     Workshops for cutting, welding, tooling, etc.
-     Foundry operations (iron, aluminum, copper, etc.).
-     Prime movers family repair workshops for electric motor, pumps, compressor, fans, capacitors, valves, fuses, etc.
-     The internal combustion engine (the automobile engine) repair workshop.
-     Industrial plants: refineries, petrochemicals, gas, etc.
-     Presses: hydraulic and pneumatic systems.
-     Water treatment and distribution plants.
-     Refrigeration and air-conditioning systems workshops.

81

- Electricity generating and distributing systems: generators, transmission systems, wiring of houses, etc.
- Transportation systems: automobile, railways, ferry/water boats, airplanes, etc.
- Farm machines: lawn mowers, tractors, planters, harvesters, etc.
- Laboratories: glass blowing, microscopes, telescopes; voltmeters/ammeters, electrical bridges, weighing bridges, wristwatches, clocks and chronometers, resistance boxes, etc.
- Health care machinery/equipment: x-ray, ultra-sound, other diagnostic and monitoring devices.
- Office machines: copiers, printing presses, typewriters, computers, etc.
- Industrial machines: spinning, weaving, and sewing machines; paper-making machines, woodworking machines; etc.
- Communication systems: analog and digital telephones, GSM, radio, television/video, etc.
- Construction: housing, dams, roads, etc.
- Chemical systems: various chemical operations, battery making/charging, etc.
- Others.

The study of the listed systems and others in a developing or consuming economy would enable the vanguards to know and understand their economy and how it works. Today, Nigerians do not know their economy filled with the black boxes that have been imported over the decades under the pretext of industrialization. As a people know their economy they will then be able to deal with the problems in it.

Will the University Graduate Agree to Learn from Artisan/Craft Workshop, Factory Floor?

The Nigerian university graduates will do anything reasonable. The above question has been examined on the field. Ogbimi (1991), found that about ninety per cent of the artisans and fresh engineers in the National Youth Service Corps (NYSC) studied believed that the interaction between the university graduate and artisans/craftsmen in the craftsmen/artisans' workshops, factory floor work settings and other places where opportunities for acquiring practical skills abound is the solution to Nigerian's economic problems. Nigerian young engineers and scientists would work with artisans/craftsmen for mutual benefits. This mutually beneficial interaction would be accepted by all wise youths.

8

LINKING EDUCATION AND PRODUCTION

Many Nigerians see education as a burden today rather than see it as an asset. Those who claim that education is an asset rarely explain why it is. The principal reason for this poor perception of the place of educational institutions in national development is the poor understanding of the relevance of educational institutions in facilitating sustainable economic growth in most parts of the world.

The positive impact of education on national development has not been felt in Nigeria because education has not been linked with the rest of the economy directly. Efforts must be put up now to link education and the rest of the economy more directly in Nigeria so that the positive impact of education on national development can be realized readily.

The existing 6-3-3-4 educational system merely equips the youths with theoretical knowledge for 16 (sixteen) years and leaves them to face the frustration of joblessness and lack of career prospect. It has been explained that educational institutions in Nigeria are doing what they ought to do. Educational institutions are places of acquiring fundamental principles, whereas the rest of the economy especially the production sector should be for developing skills and pursuing life-long careers. To solve the problems of mass unemployment and low productivity and stimulate rapid industrialisation, Nigeria must set up a framework for linking education and the rest of the economy more directly, so that the youth can move uninterruptedly from educational institutions into the rest of the economy to pursue careers.

It has been explained too that for any person to develop the Relevant Production Skills (RPSs) for his society, he must acquire adequate advanced theoretical skill (TSs), practical skills (PSs) and face challenges frequently. For Nigerian university graduates who spend a minimum of 16 years to acquire fundamental principles (TSs), how long should they be trained to acquire a balanced quantity and quality of complementary practical skills and begin to think independently?

Lack of understanding of the need to acquire adequate,balanced (complementary) theoretical skills and practical skills to equip any individual with the relevant production skills is the biggest obstacle to realizing the benefits of education in the developing world, Africa in particular. The lack of understanding of the need to acquire balanced TSs and PSs underlies the organization of ineffective practical skills-acquiring training programmes. Invariably, these programmes do not impart adequate or desired skills because they only last for very short times.Besides, the programmes are not based on well articulated goal-oriented curricula. A serious defect common to all training programmes in Nigeria is that trainees are paid very poor allowances which are also paid in a very irregular manner. These reduce the interest of trainees and promote indiscipline.

Role of Training and Employment

Britain achieved the first modern Industrial Revolution (IR) in the period 1770-1850. The United States of America (USA) also achieved the modern IR in the period 1850s-1900, the same period as most other European nations. The Asian nations then followed: Japan, 1886-1905 and China, as from the 1950s. The Newly Industrialising nations – Singapore, Taiwan, South Korea, India, Malaysia, etc., entered their rapid industrialisation phase in the second half of the 20th century.

Examination of history shows that all the nations that have achieved the modern IR followed the evolutionary path because of very low learning intensity. These nations did not emphasize learning/education for a very long time. They however, emphasized education after existing for centuries as nations.

This book has presented the theory that industrialisation is a learning and capability-building process. It has also presented the theory that education must be complemented by training for the acquisition of complementary practical skills to promote rapid industrialisation. This book also presented the theory that employment is the blood of an economy – healthy economies employ many millions of knowledgeable and skilled people.

There is the need to explain the additional special roles of training and employment in promoting sustainable economic growth, industrialisation and development (SEGID). Much of the knowledge available and taught in educational institutions at the nursery, primary, secondary and tertiary levels in the poor nations of Africa, Latin America and Asia, is not applied in economic activities due to unemployment. This painful waste is responsible for the slow development in many developing nations.

Emphasizing training and employment can accelerate development for many reasons. First, anyone who possesses either of theoretical knowledge and limited practical skills, alone, is a mediocre (Ogbimi, 1991); providing adequate training for the acquisition of complementary practical skills for all graduates of educational institutions would speedily create a knowledgeable and skilled work force. Second, because knowledge and skills cannot be applied independent of the people who possess them, employment promotes, the application of existing and new knowledge in a society. We can conclude that training and employment are the fundamental bases for linking the educational sector and the rest of the economy. We can also conclude that training and employment are the principal transporters of knowledge from educational institutions. Education, training and employment are therefore, the principal tools for promoting rapid development. This explains why poverty always co-exists with mass unemployment of all categories of work force.

Setting-up a Practical Skills-Acquisition Framework

Nigeria should set up a practical-skills-acquisition framework to complement the 6-3-3-4 educational system. The new framework should be coded SSS-2-U-4 (Ogbimi, 1998). This means that graduates of the Senior Secondary School (SSS) should compulsorily spend 2 (two) years to acquire practical skills before proceeding to the university; the SSS graduate should no more be rushing into universities as immature and unskilled people. This covers the 'SSS-2' portion of the code.

On graduating from the university, having completed a 4-year programme, he or she should also undergo a 4-year practical skills training scheme. If he completes a 5-year engineering degree, his practical training should also last 5 years. This portion explains the 'U-4' portion of the new framework code.

The establishment of this practical skills-acquiring framework will link education and production directly in Nigeria. The framework would enable Nigeria to realize readily, the positive impact of education on national development. The setting up of the practical skills framework would solve mass unemployment and low productivity problems speedily and stimulate rapid industrialisation in Nigeria.

The emphasis underlying this suggestion is using the learning places in the economy to acquire complementary practical skills, the emphasis is not on employment positions. This derives from our theory that wealth creation (and achieving sustainable economic growth) is a function of the learning opportunities, learning rate, and the quantity and quality of knowledge, skills and capabilities being applied in a production system. A progressive nation therefore should be more concerned with the learning opportunities available for the youths, not employment positions for those already pursuing chosen careers. This is how rapid development can be facilitated. Good governments pursue development objectives not profit motives. While profit-seekers see employment as a by-product of profit-making, government must see employment as the blood of economy. This is what theory (foresight) and experience advise.

Solving Unemployment Problem

Unemployment problem would be solved when Nigerians are educated and trained to be versatile and highly employable. The SSS-2-U-4 framework would create educated, highly skilled, versatile, and highly employable workforce. Hitherto, Nigeria's and other African nations' manpower development programmes only go through a half cycle. The SSS-2-U-4 would ensure that youths go through a complete cycle and get balanced education and training. The individual and people who acquire balanced and adequate knowledge and skills do not experience unemployment.

The artisan is the man sustaining the Nigerian economy today. When the Nigerian science and engineering university graduates acquire the practical skills the artisan possesses and more, he would be ready to make parts of many of the machinery and equipment Nigeria imports today. The industrialization vanguard would initiate the industrialisation and expansion that would increase learning and employment opportunities dramatically.

Improving Productivity

Our theory of employment, chapter 6, showed that increase in employment (in quantity and quality) increases the knowledge, skills and capabilities being applied in production. This in turn improves productivity and reduces inflation. The SSS-2-U-4 framework would make it possible for many people to possess both theoretical and practical skills and become versatile and highly-employable. These will rapidly increase the knowledge, skills and capabilities being applied in solving problems, including production. This would rapidly improve productivity correspondingly.

Stimulating Rapid Industrialisation

From our theory of industrialisation (chapter 3) and the theory of employment, productivity and inflation (chapter 6), we know that industrialisation is a transformation. It is a transformation achieved through the discipline of learning and acquiring knowledge, skills and capabilities and applying these in solving problems. Industrial transformation entails increase in employment, increase in the knowledge, skills and capabilities being applied in a production system and increase in the experience of the workforce. Rapid transformation is facilitated by high quality workforce, high rate of learning and good breadth and depth of knowledge in a system. The SSS-2-U-4 practical skills framework would facilitate rapid industrialization in Nigeria, because it would promote the necessary conditions for it.

Our analysis suggests that a full industrial transformation would probably be achieved when 15 (fifteen) million university graduates become employed and are involved in productive activities in Nigeria. We emphasize graduates because of the sophistry of knowledge, skills and capabilities needed to achieve industrial transformation today. With the establishment of the SSS-2-U-4 framework, 20 (twenty) per cent increase in the current university output every year in twenty years would enable Nigeria achieve full industrial transformation. The positive impact of the new framework would be evident immediately it is set up and transformation would be rapid.

Remember that the main difference between African, Latin American and the poor Asian nations on one hand and European nations, America and Canada on the other hand, is that whereas the former nations are not industrialized, the latter nations are industrialized. The technologically advanced nations were not born advanced nations; they achieved the enviable status through very slow learning. African, Latin American and the poor Asian nations have no choice; they must work very hard toward achieving rapid industrialisation.

Developing the SMEs in Nigeria

Serious intellectual exercise has never been part of the development efforts in Africa, Latin America and the poor regions of Asia. Development activities in these regions have always been based on sentiments and vogue promoted by those who benefit from the stagnation, retrogression and the increasing poverty and shame in these regions, especially Africa. Latin American nations became independent nations as from the 1820s (Fagg, 1969). Following the attainment of independence by Latin American nations, one state after another lapsed into a condition of chronic disorder. Insurrection against governments received the dignifying name of revolution as if some great political principles were at stake (Fagg, 1969). The military chieftain (caudillo) who reached the presidential palace posed as the regnenerator, restorer or the real liberator of the afflicted people. In truth, he was a greedy dictator, the real successor of the imperial power without any sense of responsibility. Half-hearted efforts were made towards economic development. Such efforts were generally confined to *unduly seeking foreign investments and placing unexplained trust on the small-scale industry,* exploiting natural resources - minerals, timber, land, under the cover of land reforms, and government officials conniving with foreigners against the interest of Latin Americans. Similar half-hearted efforts were devoted to expanding education and increasing mass participation in the production process (Fagg, 1969).

African nations, especially West African nations gained independence as from the late 1950s. Ghana became independent in 1957; Nigeria became independent in 1960. The military seized power in 1963; thereafter, it was one military coup after another in Ghana. The military seized political power in 1966 in Nigeria. Thereafter too, one military group after another seized power in Nigeria. Virtually all African nations have been adopting development strategies suggested by Europeans and Americans without thinking on their own. It has been International Technology Transfer (ITT) since independence - African nations have merely been providing a conducive environment for Europeans and Americans to transfer their wealth, especially capital, technology and institutions, to make primitive people and places in Africa modern. Virtually all African nations have been implementing the Structural Adjustment Programmes (SAPs) or reforms, introduced to them by the World Bank and IMF since the early 1980s. Like Latin American nations, African nations have always been placing undue emphasis on foreign investments and unexplained trust on the small and medium scale enterprises (SMEs).

Latin America remains a non-industrialised or a pre-industrial/rural continent after more than 150 years of independence. Similarly, Africa remains the most backward and the poorest continent after about 50 years of independence. Why have the so-called emphasis on the SMEs failed to lead to sustainable growth and industrialisation in Latin American and African nations especially Nigeria? How can the growth of the SMEs be promoted in Nigeria?

SMEs are often restricted to non-primary enterprises. That is, this category of business enterprises does not include farming, fisheries or extractive industries (UNEP Industry and Environment, 2003). The European Union (EU) categorises SMEs as: micro : 1-9 employees; small : up to 49 employees; and medium sized : up to 249 employees. The Organisation for Economic Cooperation and

Development (OECD) definition for SMEs categories is: very small : up to 19 workers; small : up to 99 workers; and medium : 100-499 workers.

In Canada, USA and Mexico, definitions of small business are different for different sectors. However, definitions based on the number of workers are popular. Annual income is also used as a premise for SMEs categorisation.

In Europe and much of the rest of the world outside Africa, most SMEs are micro in size. Most of the SMEs are in the tertiary of service sector. A 2001 survey of European SMEs (which monitors the 15 EU Member States, Iceland, Liechtenstein, Norway and Switzerland), showed that 25% of SMEs were involved in manufacture and construction. The remaining were in wholesale and retail commerce, transport and communication, and business and personal service (Observatory of European SMEs, 2001). Many countries have identified an SMEs sub-category, small and medium industries (SMIs), which generally means manufacturing/construction firms. Is that the case in the developing nations?

In OECD countries, 95% of businesses are SMEs and 60-70% of jobs are in these businesses. In 1998, 66% of jobs and 46% of businesses in the USA were estimated to be in SMEs. In 1998, of the 118.3 million enterprises surveyed in Europe, 34% were micro in size, 19% small, 13% medium and 34% were large enterprises, with 6 persons per enterprise. Of the 108.1 million enterprises surveyed in the USA in 1998, 11% were micro in size, 19% small, 16% medium and 54% large enterprises with the average number of persons per enterprise as 19. A 1996 survey of 57.3 million Japanese business enterprises showed that 33% were SMEs while 67% were large firms and the number of persons per enterprise was 10 (European Observatory of SMEs, 2001).

SMEs account for over half of India's GDP. About 51% of shipped manufactured goods in Japan are produced by SMEs. SMEs employed about 60% of Poland's workforce in 1995 (UNEP Industry and Environment, 2003).

Brazil defines a micro-enterprise as one with up to 19 employees and a small enterprise as one with between 19 and 99, with annual gross income under 1.5 million reals ($0.5 million) in each case (Barros, et al., 2003). There are about 4 million micro and small enterprises in Barazil. The vast majority are in the service and commercial (retail) sector. Most are located in the South-East region (55.5%) followed by the South (22.4%) and North (1.3%). According to the IBGE (Brazilian Geographical and Statistical Bureau), the micro and small enterprises are choosing to locate in the South-East region in order to benefit from its wider market variet, better urban infrastructure, more qualified workforce and larger consumer market (43% of the population lives in this region). In so doing, they are following the same trend as medium and large companies. In many cases, micro and small enterprises depend on or are complementary to medium and large businesses. They supply goods and services to larger firms or serve as niche markets. They are usually subcontractors, operating in networks consisting of the main large and medium companies and their clients, suppliers contractors and competitors.

Business generated in the service and retail sectors represents around 80% of the total activities of Brazil's micro and small enterprises, according to IBGE report based on the 2001 data. The report also found out that 2 million enterprises of that size in the service and retail sectors hired 7.3 million people in the study year, representing 9.7% of Brazil's total employed population. Between 1985 and 2001, these enterprises employment grew from 3.5 million(50.7% of total employment in this sector) to 7.3 million or 60.8% of the sector's workforce. The report also revealed that the areas strongly represented among the micro and small retail businesses inculded textiles and clothing, jewellery-making, watch-making and construction materials. The IBGE report stated that Brazil's GNP had reached R$570 billion (US$200 billion), with a population of over 170 million. Brazil's main industrial activities are the production of consumer goods and agricultural and mineral products for export, the report added.

The description and categorisation of SMEs in Brazil are patterned after those in the West. They are commonly based on the number of employees and the annual income of the business enterprises. It is the same approach in Asia. Unfortunately, these quantitative indices do not necessarily indicate the intrinsic values of the enterprises. Hence, they also do not constitute an appropriate basis for the management of the SMEs. For example an SME enterprise that employs 1-9 employees is a micro enterprise in EU, whereas a micro enterprise in Brazil may employ up to 19 workers. Yet, the output or income of a micro enterprise in EU- a post-industrial region, may be much higher than that of a small enterprise in Latin America - a pre-industrialised region. It is therefore not proper to claim that SMEs in all parts of the world have great potential in terms of output and the employment they provide. After all, one-man enterprise like the tyre vulcanizer or welder is an SME. What is the potential of the vulcanizer or welder in terms of output and employment in Nigeria? Unfortunately, the management of the SMEs in Nigeria has always been viewed in terms of vogue and erecting more sturctures through capital investment.

In Nigeria, the belief is that SMEs are the hope for the nations's industrialisation, because SMEs provide most of the jobs and are also responsible for virtually all the businesses in other parts of the world. It is all a matter of vogue. It is also a matter of capital investments and erecting sturctures so that SMEs in Nigeria can immediately begin to play the roles they are claimed to be playing in other nations. To the Nigerian expert, the development of the SMEs requires two things. First, erection of infrastructure by government. Second, the investment of capital by individuals, groups and organisations. A review of Nigeria's experience withs respect to the SMEs shows these features quite clearly.

Nigeria has been planning for the rapid development of the SMEs since the late 1960s. The 1970-74 Second Nation Development Plan (Federal Ministry of Finance and Economic Planning, 1970), emphasized the need to develop the SMIs. According to Ebong (2006), successive governments in Nigeria have attempted to address the myriad of problems militigating against enhanced production in the SMEs sector to enable it contribute optimally to economic growth in the nation. The initiatives included the establishment of the Nigerian Industrial Development Bank; the establishment of the Nigerian Bank of Commerce and Industry; before the deregulation of the financial service sector, banks were required to channel a minimum proportion of their credit portfolio to the preferred sectors, including SMEs; the Rural Banking Scheme; the World

Bank assisted SME I (1985) & II (1989) Loan Projects; the establishment of the Peoples Bank; the Family Economic Advancement Programme (1997), and the establishment of the Nigerian Agricultural Cooperative Bank.

The most recent initiative designed to promote the growth of the SMEs in Nigeria, Ebong continued, is the Small and Medium Enterprises Equity Investment Scheme (SIMEEIS). The SMEEIS is a contribution of the banking industry to the reform of the Federal government. It is an equity created from the contribution of 10% of the profits before tax of all banks. According to Ebong (2006), there were many other financial initiatives aimed at developing the SMEs in Nigeria. These included the National Economic Reconstruction Fund (NERFUND) and the African Development Bank's Export Stimulation Loan Scheme (ADB-ESL).

What was the state of the SMEs in the 1960s-1970s and how has the various financial initiatives transformed the SMEs and SMIs? Is there any evidence that the SMEs and SMIs in Nigeria play the roles they are claimed to be playing in the industrialised world?

Aluko, et al. (1972, 1973), studied 27,343 SMIs in Nigeria. The types of industries involved were: (1) Bakery, (2) Blacksmithing, (3) Bicycle repairing, (4) Brewering, (5) Brick making, (6) Carving, (7) Carpentry, (8) Drum-making, (9) Dyeing, (10) Electricals, (11)Furniture-making, (12) Grain milling, (13) Gold smithing, (14) Knitting, (15) Mat-making, (16) Motor repairing, (17) Printing, (18) Saw-milling, (19) Shoe-making, (20) Spinning/Weaving, (21) Tailoring, (22) Watch repairing, (23) Welding and (24) Miscellaneous. Thus, the scope of industrial units involved in the study was quite broad and reflected the true or real indigenous skills and efforts aimed at learning and promoting true growth, industrialisation and development. Aluko, et al. (1972, 1973), defined a small scale industry as one whose total assets in capital equipment and plant and working capital are less than N25,000.00 and employs fewer than 50 full time workers and it included factory or nonfactory establishments and it may be a household, a cottage, a craft or a factoryindustry. SMIs, according to these authors, may or may not use motive power.

The authors concluded that the obstacles to the rapid growth of the SMIs were:

(i)   Shortage of basic infrastructure
(ii)   Entrepreneurial and management skills
(iii)   Technical problems
(iv)   Staff training
(v)   Marketing problems
(vi)   Financial problems.

Ogbimi (1992), reanalysed the data collected by Aluko, et al. (1972, 1973) and revealed that 35.6% of the people in the SMIs in Nigeria in the 1970s were illiterates, 55.5% had primary school education, 8.8% had modern school/ secondary school education, while 0.1% had university education. With this quality of workforce, the SMIs were not ready for the needed transformation. The average educational background of the workforce in the SMIs must be increased substantially to promote rapid development in the sector. Ogbimi (1992), however, revealed that the great potential of the SMIs in Nigeria in the 1960s and 1970s was in promoting high intensity-learning. Whereas 37% of the workforce was self-employed, 12.5% worked for wages and 50.5% was apprentices. The average apprenticeship period was 3.5 years. The growth potential of the SMIs in the cirvumstance was modelled as:

$$V_N = 2^{N/3.5} V_0 \dots\dots\dots\dots\dots\dots (9)$$

where V_0 is the value of the industry at a particular time, V_N is the value any future time N. This is a very high growth potential. V_N will be twice the value of V_0 in 3.5 years, four times in 7 years and eight times in 10.5 years. The potential of the SMIs is not so much in providing permanent jobs as in teaching apprentices and generating new units, if well managed. It is this high growth potential that a young nation like Nigeria should exploit.

Unfortunately, the intellectuals, intelligentsia and business people who have been influencing economic policies for decades in Nigeria, erroneously believe that mere capital investment is the primary source of sustainable economic growth and industrialisation (SEGI). They therefore claim that capipital investments (infrastructure, marketing problems, financial problem, etc.) are the obstacles to the development of the SMEs in Nigeria. Capitalistic intellectuals and intelligentsia do not understand the human development process, hence they claim that scarcity of investment capital is the main obstacle to developing the SMIs in Nigeria.

The Executive Summary of the 2004 Baseline Economic Survey of Small and Medium Scale Industries in Nigeria, prepared by the Nigerian Institute of Social and Economic Research (NISER), Ibadan and various universities and submitted to the Central Bank of Nigeria (CBN), was based on the assumption that the main obstacle to the development of the SMEs in Nigeria is limited access to investment capital. The openning sentence of the introduction read:

It has been recognised that among the constraints to effective development of SMIs in Nigeria is limited access of the investors to long-term credit and the general non-availability of a comprehensive information which can guide potential investors and, hence, reduce the cost of pre-investment information gathering which may be very high and prohibitive.

The units surveyed therefore were not the indigenous types studied by Aluko, et al. in the 1970s. Rather, they were those that largely make up the Manufacturers Association of Nigeria (MAN): Food, Beverage and Tobacco; Textiles, Wearing Apparel and Leather Products; Wood and Wood Products; Pulp, Paper and Paper Products; Non-Metallic Mineral Products; Electrical and Electronics; Basic Metal, Iron and Steel and Fabricated Metal Products; Motor Vehicle and Miscellaneous Assembly; Plastic and Rubber Products; Information and Communication Technology; Solid Minerals Mining/Processing; and Others.

The surveyed enterprises were sub-divided into small and medium scale based on the number of persons employed. Enterprises employing between 10 and 50 persons were regarded as small scale whereas those employing between 51 and 300 persons were considered to be medium scale. Of a total of 6,344 questionaires administered to operators in the nation, 4,462, representing 70.3 per cent, returned questionnaires. Empirical analysis revealed that 4185 operators (94.1%) fell into the small scale category while 262 (5.9%) were in the medium scale category. Over 40 per cent of the SMIs were sole propietorship enterprises, about 30 per cent were limited liability companies, 12 per cent were partnership, while 7 per cent cooperative enterprises. The number of people employed by the SMIs were 53,686 while the number of people employed by the medium scale enterprises was 40,130. The total number of people employed by the 4,462 small and medium enterprises surveyed was 93,816. Hence there were an average of 21 employees per enterprise. Permanent employment accounted for most employment nationally. The proportion of permanent employment however, varied from 37% in the Wood & Wood Products sector to the highest of 57% in the Information and Communication Technology Sector. Nationally, 5% of the persons in the SMEs in the Solid Minerals Mining/Processing sector - the lowest among all the sectors were apprentices, while 19% of the persons in the Basic Metals, Iron & Steel and Fabricated Products sector - the highest among all the sectors were apprentices. Nationally, too, the distribution of skilled categories appeared relatively even among skilled, semi-skilled and unskilled. The survey showed that most of the SMIs sourced their most important raw materials both locally and from abroad; most of the materials sourced locally were imported products. In other words, most of the SMIs surveyed import their inputs - an indication that they do not add significant value in their production process.

It is clear that there is a problem as to how to manage the SMEs in Nigeria. There are at least two aspects to the problem of how to manage the SMEs. First, which group of SMEs should the nation emphasize - is it the indigenous group made up of Bakery, Blacksmithing, Bicycle repairer, Brick making, Carving, Electrical, Motor repairing, etc., the types Aluko, et al. (1972, 1973), sudied, or those who are members of the Manufacturers Association of Nigeria - the Food, Beverage and Tobacco; Textiles; Wearing Apparel and Leather Products; Pulp, Paper and Paper Products, etc.? Second, what should the focus be - is it the capital invested on them rather than on the high learning intensity feature of the indigenous SMIs?

Our growth theories in this book show clearly that industrialisation is a learning and capability-building process. Consequently, it is the high learning intensity feature of the SMEs that Nigeria should focus on and not on the amount of capital invested on them. Mere capital investment does not promote sustainable economic growth and industrialisation.

Nigeria is an artisan/craft economy, the endowment of oil wealth notwithstanding, the SMEs in Nigeria cannot be managed the same way as those in the United States of America, Japan and Europe. In the reviews above, while 108.1 million and 57.3 million enterprises respectively, were surveyed in the United States and Japan, 4 million were surveyed in Brazil and only 4300 enterprises were surveyed in Nigeria. Is the Nigerian case comparable to that of the United States and Japan? Not at all. Is it even comparable to the Brazilian situation? No.

African leaders (intellectuals and intelligentsia, the politician, the business people) do not see the need to think before acting. The African only have to hear what was said in Europe, America and Asia and begin to sing it as an axiomatic truth. Obong (2006), reflecting on the Nigerian SMEs situation wrote:

The need to role back the frontiers of government and allow the private sector to spearhead the economic growth and development process has been recognised by policy makers in Nigeria. Accordingly, the government has since embarked on the privatisation of public enterprises. Under this arrangement, the public sector is only expected to provide an enabling environment for private business to thrive. Essentially, the role of government in the developiment process is limited to the provision of law and order as well as basic infrastructure required for the efficient functioning of the private sector. Resource allocation will, therefore be primarily determined by the signals emanating from the market. In this model, the small and medium -

scale enterprises (SMEs) sector is expected to play a leading role in terms of contribution to major economic indicators like gross domestic product and employment.

Obong (2006), continuing, added. *The attempt to rely on SMEs to drive accelerated economic growth in Nigeria is also borne out of the experience with large-scale enterprises. The operations of these enterprises did not rob off significantly on the Nigerian economy in terms of the benefits that had been anticipated largely because they depended heavily on imported inputs. Priority is being assgned to the SME sector based on the experiences of other countries. In China, for instance, SMEs account for about 60% of industrial output and about 75% of the workforce in urban centre.*

For SMEs to generate desired outcomes, however, it is crucial that the constraint facing them are comprehensively addressed. The factors that have made it difficult to fully realise the potentials of the sector in Nigeria, include infrastructural deficiencies, unstable macroeconomic environment and poor access to finance.

Having listed many of the efforts government put up over the decades to promote SMEs, Obong (2006), concluded sadly, that the measures and initiatives yielded limited results for many reasons. Notable among the reasons were the problems posed by inadequate infrastructure. The epileptic power supply situation is a classic example.

Ogbimi (1992), observed that the Nigerian case is one of trying to put the cart before the horse or refusing to reason. The Nigerian case is also one where greed is frustrating reasoning. In a situation where greed is frustrating reasoning, there cannot be a correct perception of the problems confronting a society.

Poor perception and definition of a problem precludes finding the true solution. That situation may be likened to that in which a tourist is given a tour guide in which there is an error at a point; the tourist is erroneously directed to go west instead of east. Under that circumstance, the more the efforts the tourist makes, the farther away he becomes from the point he should really be approaching. Except that error is corrected, the tourist's effort would be causing him more problems.

The foregoing scenario seems to describe the Nigeian situation during the past five decades. Many African nations were able to feed themselves and did not owe anyone in the 1960s and 1770s. But the situation after many African nations became politically independent in the early 1960s, became one of falling from grace to grass. And the promises and hopes at independence have been replaced with fighting for survival, anxiety and hopelessness.

It can only be that African leaders are going west instead of east as in the above scenario, or more technically, having poor perception and definition of the problems facing their societies. The solution to the error of going west instead of east is a full turn through 180 degrees to the opposite direction. Africa's hope lies in turning from the direction of hopelessness and gloom to that of hope and happiness.

Thirty years after the invention of the automobile in 1886, 198 different brands of it were made and introduced into market in Europe (Turner, 1963). Compare that situation with that in Africa in which the automobile has been introduced for more than fifty years with no single indigenous brand manufactured and not even reliable maintenance capabilities acquired. Is it because Africans are unintelligent? Before 1300, the level of scientific and technological achievements in Europe in many respects was lower than that of the great civilization of China, India, and the Islamic world. In those civilizations, science had flourished during the Dark Ages of the West. It is claimed that the West caught up with the then advanced cultures in science in 1300, but the West did not immediately make the great scientific strides that it later showed it is capable of making, and therefore, there was a centuries-long plateau between absorption of the oriental knowledge and an independent Western science (Gottschalk, et al., 1969). Was that because the West was not intelligent then?

In the two instances, it is neither because Africans were unintelligent nor the West was unintelligent. It was all because of the nature of technologoy and technological development, which may be likened to a ladder-climbing process in which essential steps and sequence cannot be omitted (Ogbimi, 1990). It is also a learning process like piano-playing, where the talented must first learn the ordinary tunes before composing independent tunes to show his talent. One who devotes much effort towards learning acquires knowledge and skills rapidly. One who has a teacher, or one who has the opportunity to learn from the experiences of others and tries things out on his own before seeking genuine assistance, progresses rapidly; one who does not learn cannot acquire knowledge and skills. Societies mutually influence each other in technological development, for no society became advanced in isolation (Ogbimi, 1988).

Apparently, many Africas do not realize these so as to place problems in their proper perspectives. The West learnt from Africa and Asia in the medieval times; it is the turn of Africa to learn from the West. The student must be guided by his own instinct and experience to maximize his gains from the encounter this time around; Europe did so earlier on.

Economic development is misconceived in Africa. One dimension of this misconception is that, African planners see the predominantly artisan/craftman business enterprises in Africa in the light of Western multinational corporations like International Business Machines (IBM) of America, General Motors Corporation of America, Unilever of the United Kingdom, Mercedez Benz of Germany, etc. Unfortunately, we know that feeding adult diet to a one-month old baby can only be a grievous mistake which when continued for an extended time may cause irreversible damages.

Multinational corporations are certainly important organisation which contribute immensely to the economic well-being of citizens in the West. But it must not be forgotten that they are not the products of two days activities; they have been nurtured for centuries. Africa can transform its production structure rapidly but not by mere capital investements. Rapid transformation can be done by avoiding those things that delayed the development of 'older' societies and doing the growth-promoting things they did not do, which careful studies have indicated would accelerate African economic development.

If one considers the basic fact that present multinational corporations began as one or two-persons' entrepreneurial activities at a time no one acquired knowledge and skills aggressively, and many centenarians could not read or write, as against the situation today, where five-year old kids read and write, Africa can reduce the time for transforming its production structure by a factor of 40 when compared with the time it took Europe to learn from Africa and Asia. All it needs is knowing what to do and doing it.

The birth of the automobile is usually claimed to be 1886, the year Karl Benz and Daimler came out with their car (Monadori, 1985). The history of Mercedes Benz and other automobile multinationals therefore, began thereafter. But the activities connected with the invention of the automobile date back to the discovery of the power of the atmospheric pressure in 1643 by Evangelista Torricelli and the subsequent design of the steam engine, the precursor of the internal combustion engine by Newcomen and Cawley, one a blacksmith and the other a glazier. The artisan/craftsman activities which gave birth to the automobile thus, evolved for more than 240 years before the invention of the automobile in 1886. It is important to remember that there has always been a nurturing stage in any industrialisation quest and it seems it cannot be omitted.

At the time Europeans were dreaming about a car, they had no one to build complex plants which could give the illusion that they can take short cut in development. They, therefore, had to depend on their 'engineer' and 'scientist'.

All histories of human development endeavours have also consistently shown that human resource and the development of the capabilities to build new tools, machinery and equipment are the keys to economic development. Drucker (1957) said that only man is capable of enlargement, because man grows, develops and acquires skills. Unfortunately, human resources have not always received the serious attention they deserve as crucial determinants of economic develoment. The 1960s and early 1970s in particular, witnessed a widespread fallacy which explained economic development in terms of capital and treated human resources as a non-essential factor (UNIDO, 1989).

After a brief speel of living under the influence of an unfortunate fallacy, it has become widely accepted again that it is human beings and the skills they command that are the decisive factors in promoting economic development and industrialisation. There is an increasing awareness that it is the education and skill level of the labour force which determine a nation's competitive strength and resilience, its capacity to adjust to new technologies and to reduce the economic and social cost of change.

The poor performance of the Nigerian economy and the small scale industry today, five decades after the emphasis on the sector commenced, suggests poor perception and definition of the small scale industries' problems and consequently the inappropriate strategies designed for developing the SMEs in Nigeria. First, the nomenclature small, medium and large scale industries is actuqally, a 'solution lost in elegance' (SLE) approach to describing the situation. It is SLE because although the nomenclature sounds elegant, it conceals the problems which the African need to address to improve his productivity.

If the nomenclature artisan/craft, mechanized and automated production systems were adopted, the problems of the present African production system, the artisan/craft production system would readily be brought to mind. Artisan/craft activities are characterized by the exertion of human muscles. Improvement in productivity in it would require building machines to do some of the work the African does manually; the production process would need to be mechanized. However, as was noted earlier on, mechnization of the African production system cannot be done by mere capital investment. For, the education and skills of the labour force are the determinants of a country's competitive strength and ease of adjusting to new technologies.

But because Nigeria has been living under the influence of the late 1960s and early 1970s fallacy that capital is the basis of economic development and human resources are unimportant, it stucked to the SLE approach. And what is small scale industry under the SLE nomenclature? Nigeria, India, the United States and all other nations and regions of the world have different definitions of their own though most of these definitions are based on the annual income or fixed capital of the enterprises and the nominal number of employees. The common basis of the different definitions does not distinguish between the African artisan/craftsman enterprises and those in the technologically developed world.

Since the fundamental basis of Western economic theory is the fallacious claim that capital investments promote sustainable economic growth, and African intellectuals and intelligentsia do not have any thought of their own yet, the claim by Western and African experts about the lack of growth of the SMEs in the continent is that not enough capital has been invested in the sector. However, Western and African experts are wrong. No amount of mere capital investment promotes growth; no amount of capital investment in the SMEs in Africa including Nigeria will stimulate sustainable growth in the sector.

Yet, African leaders and the Western and African experts who advise them will not stop the promotion of capital investment in Africa. This is for three or more reasons. First, they do not understand the human development process, hence they believe that mere capital investment will transform the African artisan/craftman enterprises into the type of big enterprises common in the West and Asia especially Japan and Korea today. Second, the African leader and his experts do not believe that the African indigenous artisan/craftsman enterprise can be transformed into bigger and technologically advanced enterprises, hence they are always campaigning for foreign investments especially Foreign Direct Investments (FDIs) through which more advanced enterprises would be erected to supplant the undesirable indigenous ones.

Third, unknown to the ignorant African, the African leader and his Western and African advisers are quite aware that mere capital investment does not promote sustainable economic growth and industrialisation (SEGI. But the African leader and his Western and African advisers are exploiting the ignorant and gullible African by emphasizing capital investments, seeking foreign investments, aid, and loans unnecessarily, and erecting structures indiscriminately.

Many Africans, both educated in the Western way and those uneducated, probably do not know that the good roads, good transport systems including metroline,railways, airplanes, electricity, potable water, good drainage systems, good health systems and indeed good refuse disposal systems in the West, are fruits or aftermath of industrialisation. African leaders and their advisers are unable to distinguish between the cause and effect, they are unable to understand that industrialisation is the cause of the good and reliable utilities and wealth in the West. Consequently, Africans believe that by securing loans and erecting structures such as road and tellecommunication networks, industrial plants, advanced hospitals, dams, electric power generating plants and distributing systems, transport systems including fleet of vehicles and railways, urban centres and real estate, etc., and by erecting airports and seaports and buying planes and ships/ocean liners, the airtisan/caraft African economies would be transformed overnight into advanced societies. Putting this in another way, Africans think that they can enjoy the fruits of industrialisation first, before embarking on the industrialisation process that will transform the artisan/craft African economies into technologicall advanced ones.

Africans are very wrong in their conception of the human development process. Human beings achieve puberty before they are able to procreate; human beings do not procreate before they achieve puberty. The African leaders and their people cannot appear to be walking head-down and thinking with the stomach and expecting to achieve progress. It also appears that some people are benefiting from the African retrogressing.

Who is gaining from the African retrogression and why is the effort to sustain the African retrogression gaining increasing momentum? The African leaders and thier Western and African advisers, Western nations and institutions, foreign investors and the African business people - the private sector, are the individuals and groups that are gaining from the African retrogression. They are the people working very hard to sustain the things that are promoting the African retrogression. How?

The African leader who awards the highly inflated contracts for erecting roads and telecommunication networks, dams, drainage systems, and for various procurements and supplies, receive both demanded and undemanded kick-backs. The Western and African experts who claim to know what they do not know and sustain the deceit that Africa is achieving phenomenal growth and development through propaganda, is paid heavily for his economic-man role. Westerners who claim to invest in Africa to save the most backward continent and people, get unprecedented returns on their investments. The phony businesss enterprises they set up in Africa easily secure foreign currencies from African governments to support their exploitative trade in Africa.

Western governments and institutions lure African nations into debt-traps through which they milk the weak nations and force them to adopt programmes that lack growth elements. Christian Aid (2006), a charity organisation, criticized Britain for taking away N6.8 trillion (E27 billion) in one year July 2005-July 2006 from sub-Saharan Africa. Britain had pledged to help Africa during the G-8 meeting in July 2006. Nigeria for example, according to Obasanjo (2006), was only owing US$0.57 billion in 1970. In 1979 when he left office as a military Head of State, Nigeria's debts were US $3.2 billion. The debt stock rose to US $18.5 billion in 1985. By 1986, Nigerian leaders in connivance with Western powers adopted the African Structural Adjustment Programmes (SAPs), programmes that lacked growth elements. In 1995, Nigeria's debt stock had risen to US $34.1 billion. In 2002, it was reduced to US $30.99 billion. In 2005, the debt stock went up to about US $39.9 due largely to interest, surcharges and penalties. Between 1992 and 2000, principal arrears on Nigeria's national debts was US $10.31 billion; interests arrears were US $4.45 billion; and late interest was US $5.18 billion. By the end of 2003, new arrears of US $3.78 billion were added in addition to principal areas of US $1.22 billion, interest arrears of US $2.4 billion and late interest of US $0.2 billion.

Okonjo-Iweala (2005), as Minister of Finance, observed that after Nigeria had paid over US $40 billion to the Paris Club and other Western creditors, the nation's foreign debts stock was still over US $35 billion. In the period 2006-2007, following the substantial revenue realised from sales of crude petroleum due to high prices of world crude petroleum, Nigeria paid about US $20 billion to Western creditors as a deal to exit from Western debt-traps. That is how the West has been milking Nigeria and other African nations.

Is it true that Nigeria has exitted from Western debt-traps? It may be Nigeria is leaving Western debt-traps into the Asian ones. After all, Nigerian leaders have been the same people since the late 1960s. While the Obasanjo regime 1999-2007 claims credit for exitting Nigeria from Western debt-trap, the same government has already negotiated a loan of US $8.3 (eight billion, three hundred million United States dollars) from China for constructing and restructuring new and old railways systems to link iron and steel plants and sea ports. This is not the first time Nigeria is securing foreign loans for constructing and modernising railways systems. They have never yielded the desired results. The same thing would happen in relation to this new debt-trap debt from China. It is being secured because of poor leadership.History will tell.

China used to depend on the Union of the Soviet Socialist Republic (USSR) for the erection of infrastructure including railways, but China did not have a reliable infrastructural network till China herself developed the relevant competence to build and sustain appropriate infrastructure (Stokes and Stokes, 1975). The debt that Nigeria is securing from China is an unwise one. It is the beginning of the evil days with the Asians.

What Nigeria needs to do is to stop securing loans and awarding inflated contracts for erecting complex infrastructure. All resources should be mobilized for developing the relevant knowledge and skills and achieving industrialisation in Nigeria.

Nigeria should stop adopting development strategies and programmes based on vogue. Nigerians need to build a nation and an economy. When Nigerians have done these, they may then get involved in politics and jokes of which ideology Nigeria can adopt. No ideology per se, solves the common problems that confront a technologically backward and poor nation. Rapid technological growth saved the United states of America (Bulletin of S & T and Culture, 1984). It is also rapid technological growth that can save Nigeria. No amount of capital investments will save Nigeria.

Nigerian politicians and experts, for decades, have been claiming that inadequate capital and the poor status of Nigerian infrastructure have been the obstacles to the developments of the SMEs in Nigeria. It has been demonstrated unequivocally in this book that mere capital investment cannot promote sustainable economic growth and industricalisation (SEGI). Nigerian experience after uncountable financial initiatives aimed at developing the SMEs to no avail, is a practical proof of our theory.

The poor performance of infrastructure especially electric power generation and distribution is a natural consequence of a faulty development strategy. Again, the development of efficient transport and telecommunication systems, electric power generating and distribution systems, availability of potable water systems, etc., in the West is a fruit of or aftermath of the industrialisation there. They cannot be developed by mere capital investment. The performance of infrastructure is determined by the technological competence of a society.

The performance of SMEs in an artisan economy like Nigeria's cannot be assessed in isolation. To promote rapid technological growth in Nigeria, Nigeria must emphasize learning especially education and training. Education for all through primary, secondary and tertiary levels would equip the youth with the necessary theoretical knowledge, developed minds and character. All graduates of educational institutions should be given training for the acquisition of complementary practical skills. University science and engineering graduates should receive 3-4 years training for the acquisition of practical skills in artisan/craftsman workshops, factory floor worksettings and all other places where opportunities for acquiring practical skills abound. They should be paid adequate allowances during the training period so as to keep interest and discipline high. This is how the Nigerian economy including the SMEs can be transformed rapidly.

Promoting Rapid Capability-building Agricultural Development in Nigeria

Agriculture is very important to the well-being of the citizens of a nation. This is because it includes, among other things, raising crops and animals, fish farming, hunting, food processing and distribution, and management of forest resources. When these roles are efficiently played, agriculture provides food of suitable quantity and quality; it provides respectable employment; it supplies industrial and construction materials; and forms an important basis of a rewarding international trade.

Apparently, only advanced agricultural systems play the foregoing roles. For whereas the British and other European systems, the American and Japanese ones play virtually all the roles listed above and more, Nigeia's agriculture remains an artisan/craft and low-productivity one, unable to play any of the roles listed above, 47 years after the commencement of the efforts put up by various government and international organisations to develop it. Why have the various efforts to develop Nigeria's agriculture not yielded the desired results?

We recall the injunction, 'think before you act', it warns us that except our thoughts about the solution to a problem is correct, we shall not be able to slove it. Nigeria's thoughts about the development of her artisan agriculture are not correct. Hence, the activities thereof are also incapable of producing the desired results.

Nigeirans think that a nation may achieve or develop advanced agriculture in a primitive economy. Nigeria leaders (intellectuals/intelligentsia, politicians and business men and women) probably do not know that advanced agriculture is a fruit or an aftermath of industrialisation. This means that Nigerians do not know that just as there is precedence in the human development process (all human beings achieve puberty before they become part of procreation), so there is precedence in the development of human societies (societies achieve industrialisation before economic diversification - the economic status in which all the sectors of an economy including the agricultural sector begin to perform efficiently). Nigerian leaders are also unable to see that competence cannot be purchased like a commodity; hence, mere capital investments do not promote sustainable economic growth and industrialisation (SEGI).

Consequently, Nigeria's industrialisation and agricultural development endeavours for about 50 years so far, have been characterized by mass importation of complex machinery and equipment and erection of complex infrastructure. These efforts can neither promote industrialisation nor transform the artisan agriculture into an advanced one. Government continues to measure quantitative growth in agriculture in Nigeria. This is growth due to expansion of cropped areas by small holders farmers rather than increase in productivity. Mr. Ordu Obibiaku (2005), British Department for International Development (DFID), in a paper entitled, *Agricultural Entrepreneurship Development: The Roadmap to Nigeria's Economic Diversification*, in Ilorin, Kwara State, posited that in the period 1999-2003, agriculture grew 4.6% which seemed a positive trend. However, a closer examination revealed that the increase was due to increase in farmed land. Cropped area expanded 32%, decreased yield resulted in low (20%) in output. This is not what Nigeria needs. International organisations continue to make the mistake that mere capital investment in artisan agriculture can be the road to achieving economic diversification in a nation, as the title of the paper delivered by Mr. Ordu Obibiaku of British DFID tended to suggest. What is the experience of the technologically advanced nations?

The region now occupied by Britain, France, Italy, Spain and Portugal had enjoyed a peaceful reign of over 400 years of the Roman empire before the western portion of the empire broke up in 406 A.D. (Carrington and Jackson, 1954). The Islands of England metamorphosed into the Kingdom of England in the tenth century (Brooke, 1968). During this eleven centuries, hoe, axe and draught oxen were the most advanced mechanization instruments of the people of the region (Davies, 1069). England and Scotland formed the Union of Great Britain in 1625.

British agriculture remained primitive till the nineteenth century. Ernle (1822), in his influential treatise on British agriculture, *English Farming Past and Present*, identified the period 1780-1813 as one of exceptional activities in agricultural development in England. Thus, for about 2000 years, the English people were tied to primitive agriculture. It is possible that many people including agricultural engineers, know this historical fact, but it is not this history per se, that is pertinent here. Rather, it the explanation for the 2000 years it took to modernise the British agricultural system and its implication for the transformation of the Nigerian artisan agriculture into an advanced one (Ogbimi, 1994b). Even more important is the understanding that the Bristish experience was typical among its contemporaries.

The relevant developments during the period of exceptional activities in British agriculture were the spread of the knowledge of improved practices and wider application of learning (Johnston and Kilby, 1979). The general level of farming was however still backward in 1846 (Jones, 1967). Britain achieved very high productivity changes which were later referred to as Industrial Revolution (IR) in the period 1770-1850 (Amrine, et al., 1982). This shows that British industrialisation preceded the agricultural mechanization.

The American experience was not different from that of Britain. Modern United States began as British colonies in 1606. The colonies declared independence in 1776 and fought the War of Independence with Britain for about eight year, 1775-1783 (Baldwin, 1969). The economy of the United States of America (USA) in the 1820s differed only a little from what it was in the eighteenth century; the production in the period was one with more than 75 per cent of the workforce tied to agriculture (Danhof, 1969). However, the half-century 1820-1870 witnessed the establishment of a modern agricultural system. Again, agricultural modernisation and mechanisation in the USA was preceded by industrialisation. For in the famous 1851 Crystal Palace, London, Industrial Exhibition, made-in-America goods were the marvel of the show (International Businessweek, 1988). The Americans forced their entry into Japan in 1854 through the awe created by the war ship flotilla commanded by Commodore Matthew Perry (Time Magazine, 1983), demonstrating that their industrial maturity came before agricultural maturity. Europe provided an invaluable stimulus for the development of American agriculture; but experience quickly taught Americans that developments in Europe could not be successfully borrowed in toto. Thomas Moore (1801) was one of those to realise that first; he observed that Americans had not derived the advantages expected from European improvements and discoveries, and suggested that they should look inward for ways for improving agricultural productivity in the USA. Mere adoption of practices in Britain through mass importation did not mechanize USA agriculture.

The Japanese claim that their existence dates back to 600 B.C. (Hall, 1971). However, when the Americans entered Japan forcefully in 1854, Japan was still an agricultural state after about 2500 years of existing as a nation. However, the 20-year period 1886-1905 witnessed the rapid industrialisation of Japan (Hall, 1971; and Stead, 1906). Advanced agriculture in Japan was preceded by industrialisation. An ancient Japanese saying runs, *Agriculture is the nursing mother of the state*, for two thousand years agriculture was at least the occupation of the majority of the Japane people (Stead, 1906). Over 60 per cent of Japanese was still employed in agriculture in 1906.

Evidence from the experiences of Britain, USA and Japan shows that industrialisation precedes the establishment of an advanced agricultural system including mechanzation. Moreover, mechanization of agriculture took the now Technologicall yAdvanced Nations (TANs) about 2000 years. Mass importation and mere adoption did not mechanized American agriculture. The implication of these for Nigeria is that the nation is trying to develop her agriculture the wrong way and expecting good results.

To promote rapid agricutural development in Nigeria, therefore, the nation must promote rapid industrialisation first. This is because the inputs into an advanced agriculture are products or fruits of industrialisation. Farm machinery and equipment, chemicals including hebicites, fungucites, etc., are relevant inputs. Besides, agriculture is just one of the sectors in an economically diversified nation. Again, economic diversification is a fruit of industrialisation. As it has been shown in earlier sections of this book, industrialisation is a learning and capability-building process. No industrialisation, no mechanized agriculture.

9

MOBILISING RESOURCES FOR INDUSTRIALISATION

That industrialized nations in the East and West enjoy a high quality life whereas artisan African nations are poor and deprived is a common knowledge. The main difference between the rich nations of the East and West on the one hand, and the poor nations of Africa on the other hand, is that whereas African nations are not industrialised, the rich nations are industrialised. Therefore, what African nations need most is industrialisation. IndustrialiSation is highly desirable and every nation ought to work hard to achieve it. The experiences of Eastern and Western nations suggest that the benefits of industrialisation far exceed its cost. Ogbimi, (2006), also showed that whereas the inputs into industrialisation increase in an arithmetic fashion, the benefits increase in a geometric progression.

Expected Demands for Industrialiation in Nigeria

The suggested SSS-2-U-4 practical skills-acquiring framework suggested for rapid industrialisation has two phases. The U-4 phase concerns acquisition of practical skills. It should be a publicly-supported programme so as to achieve the desired objectives effectively, efficiently and speedily. Participating university graduates should be paid allowance that would enable them lead a normal working-life. This is to sustain participants' interests and discipline in the programme. Poor allowance is the bane of many training programmes in Nigeria today. Hence, the allowance must cover the cost of living and more.

This calls for a departure from the dated, unserious and insincere approach to development planning in Nigeria in the past. In the past, one government after another merely makes long speeches but only gives grudging moral and material support to education and on-the-job training activities. The cost of training an individual should now be well determined. This should be well tied to the total number of individuals to be trained each year. Any contribution by government, private organizations and individuals, should be viewed in relation to the total demand or cost for the year. Funding should no more be based on an arbitrary allocation of a percentage of annual budget but on the cost of education and training each year or period.

Setting Priorities Right

To mobilise the necessary resources for industrialisation, there is need for Nigeria to set her priorities right. Otherwise, it would appear as if industrialisation is impossible or that it is not possible to mobilise the needed resources.

It is said that where a man's interest lies there his heart is. Let a man tell you who his friends are, then you know who he is. Let a man tell you what he devotes his time to, then you know his priorities. Analyse how a nation spends its revenue, identify the emphasis in the expenditure profile and you have characterized the people and their government. Table 1, shows Nigeria's annual revenue and expenditure profiles over the period 1995 - 1999. The table was based on an exchange rate of ₦85.00 to one United States dollar.

During the period, Nigeria devoted between 1 and 4 per cent of her gross annual revenue to funding education and devoted between 15.5 – 22.6 per cent to servicing/paying questionable debts. Nigeria also paid at least 43 per cent of the proceeds from oil as the cost of exploring the oil in her soil and waters each year, to multi-national oil companies who explore and produce the oil. That was besides the degradation of the environment in the Niger Delta area where the oil deposits are, the cost of which is inestimable. Nigeria also contributed at least $2 billion

Table 1:   *Nigerian Revenue and Expenditure Profiles 1995-99*

		1995	1996	1997	1998	1999
(a)	Gross Revenue (N billion)	752.33	1033.74	1099.86	1159.95	667.7
	Oil	671.33	925.74	938.86	992.95	53.70
	Non-oil	81.00	108.00	101.00	167.00	214.00
(b)	Allocation to:					
	(i) Education (N billion)	9.80	13.35	16.84	16.84	7.71
	Education (%)	1.30	1.30	1.50	1.50	4.20
	(ii) Debts (N billion)	170.00	170.00	170.00	170.00	129.00
	Debts (%)	22.6	16.4	15.5	15.5	19.4
(c)	Crude Oil Produced (Million Barrels per Day (MBPD))	2.04	2.04	2.04	2.04	2.04
	(i) Nigeria's share (MBPD):	1.163	1.163	1.163	1.163	1.163
	(%)	57.0	57.0	57.0	57.0	57.0
	(ii) Explorer's Share (ES) (cost of technology) (MBPD)	0.877	0.877	0.877	0.877	0.877
	%	43.0	43.0	43.0	43.0	43.0
(d)	Contribution to Joint Ventures (CJV) (N billion)	170	170	170	212.5	170
(e)	Debt + ES + CJV (%)	83.6	71.3	67.7	69.8	67.9
(f)	Environmental Cost	?	?	?	?	?

Source: Adapted from Nigerian Annual Budgets.

(two billion dollars) or N170b (one hundred and seventy billion naira) each year as contribution toward joint venture (CJV) oil operations with multi-national companies. The sum of Debts payments, Explorers' Share(ES) and Contribution to Joint Venture (CJV) each year varied between 67.7-83.6 per cent of gross revenue during the period. That confirmed the estimate made by Ani (1995) that for every one dollar of crude oil earned by Nigeria, at least 95 cents is re-exported to the West. That was the situation in the military era which ended May 29, 1999. What followed; did Nigeria try to set a proper priority order?

General Ibrahim Babangida as military president in the period 1985-1993, adopted the African Structural Adjustment Programme (SAPs) in 1986. Gen. Olusegun Obasanjo (rtd) had accused President Babangida of not implementing the SAPs with a human face. General Obasanjo as military Head of State of Nigeria 1976-1979 had implemented the Nigerian Indigenisation Programme in which ownership of all foreign businesses in Nigeria were compulsorily transferred to Nigerians. Gen. Olusegun Obasanjo was dramatically elected and sworn in as the democratic President of Nigeria on May 29, 1999. His economic programme this time was not new; he retained the SAPs which President Babangida had implemented for over 7 years, 1986-1993, the Late Gen. Sani Abacha had implemented 1993-1998, and Gen. Abdulsalami Abubakar had also implemented 1998-1999. However, he later re-named SAPs the National Economic Empowerment and Development Strategy (NEEDS).

Vice-President Atiku Abubakar (1999) in an address entitled, "Nigeria: Dawn of a new day," presented in the seminar organized by the World Bank and IMF in Washington, D.C., U.S.A., September 26, 1999, said among other things that: *the Organised Private Sector (OPS) is the engine of growth in an economy; it is our resolve to make the private sector the engine of growth and this is the pillar of our economic policy.* To do this, the Obasanjo administration beginning in May 1999 put up Nigeria for sale to wealthy Nigerians and foreigners at give-a-way prices. Nigeria has been up for full privatisation and deregulation (planlessness and leaving things to market forces to determine).

What type of growth was Vice-President Abubakar talking about? What type of growth has Nigerian leaders been talking about since 1960? How does privatisation promote industrialisation?

Nigeria and other African nations as artisan/craft economies have very limited ability to solve their social and economic problems. African nations need to industrialise so that they can begin to solve their problems as the industrialised nations of the world do. Do African leaders think that privatisation will promote

African industrialisation? How will privatisation do it? African leaders need to be reminded that a European philosopher, Betrand Russell (1967), warned that extreme individualism (private capitalism) discourages the growth of science and technological capabilities, for the growth of these demand the cooperation of many people and a close knit society.

Industrialisation and development have to do with the number of people educated to maximum levels of knowledge acquisition and trained to acquire complementary practical skills. No amount of structures assembled in a society where the people are illiterate, uneducated and skills-starved, will lead to sustainable growth, industrialisation and rapid development.

President Obasanjo did not design the African SAP. African intellectuals including Nigerian intellectuals did not design the African SAPs. African nations including Nigeria have only been doing what the World Bank and IMF told them to do; Africans have been 'acting without thinking' for decades. But we have demonstrated convincingly in this book that the World Bank and IMF do not understand the science of growth and development. Consequently, they cannot design a programme that will promote African industrialisation.

The status of African economies, including Nigeria's, shows clearly that African nations have been 'planting cooked seeds.' A technologically backward nation pursuing development by awarding highly inflated contracts for the construction and erection of complex structures, is analogous to one planting cooked seeks. Such a senseless nation would increasingly be stressed. Our analysis shows that the nation would experience decreasing activities; increasing intensities of idleness, mass unemployment, high crime wave, speculation, corruption, indebtedness, poverty, etc. (see Figure 5). The nation would also be trapped in the poverty promoting cycle (PPC), see Figure 11. Nigeria and virtually all other African nations, Latin American and the backward Asian nations, are experiencing the various stress conditions which our analysis predicted. It seems that Africans have been thinking with their stomach for quite a time. Nigeria and others African nations have been wasting time and other resources for decades.

Immediately Gen. Olusegun Obasanjo (rtd.) was sworn in as the President and Commander-in-Chief of the Armed Forces of the Federal Republic of Nigeria in May 1999, he promised the World Bank and IMF that he would devote at least $3.3b (three billion, three hundred million dollars) every year to servicing Nigeria's foreign debts; Alhaji Adamu Ciroma as Minister of Finance revealed this in a British Broadcasting Corporation (BBC) Hausa Programme (see also *The Guardian*, Oct. 7, 1999, p. 17).

A report of the Central Bank of Nigeria presented by the Director-General of the Debt Management Office (DMO), Arikawe Akin (2002) said Nigeria serviced her foreign debts with $7.17 billion in three years between 1999 and 2002, confirming the revelation by Alhaji Ciroma. Arikawe (2003) in another report revealed that in the previous 18 years, Nigeria repaid a total of $33.288 billion out of its cumulative debt of about $30.991 billion as at December 2001. The Director said that research revealed that 75 per cent of the money borrowed from international institutions was contracted between 1980 and 1984; 40 per cent of the borrowed money got lost in transit.

Kayode Naiyeju (2003), the Accountant General of the Nigerian Federation reported while analyzing the performance of the 2003 budget that Nigeria's monthly deficit stands at N97 billion (about $700 million dollars). That said much about the nature of Nigeria's democratic government.

Paul Collier (2003), a Professor of Economics in Oxford University, England and a World Bank Consultant revealed that Nigerians have at least $170b (one hundred and seventy billion dollars) stolen money abroad. Collier (2003a), also disclosed that $107b (one hundred and seven billion dollars) were removed from Nigeria and taken abroad during the period 1999-2003. These revelations exposed the hypocricy of the campaign against corruption, for inflow of foreign investments and for debts forgiveness in Nigeria. The revelations are also important when viewed against the background that the Nigerian government claims that SAPs and the related instruments - deregulation, privatization, etc., are not programmes of choice – that Nigeria is forced to adopt them due to her indebtedness. The African SAPs and their dated, stress-imposing, primitive and enslaving instruments like privatization and deregulation were imposed on indebted African nations including Nigeria by Western nations and their institutions (the World Bank and IMF) in the early 1980s.

A report published by the International Institute for Strategic Studies (2001), rated Nigeria as the largest defence spender in West Africa; Nigeria in the period 1999-2003 probably spent more than $8 billion on importing arms. Will mere importation of arms establish a nation as a strong military power? Why is Nigeria importing a lot of arms to do?

What is Nigeria's plan for rescuing itself from the debt trap? Is it the SAPs that Nigeria adopted in 1986 when Nigeria's foreign debts were just about $19 billion? There has to be a plan for achieving industrialisation and improving productivity. There is none yet.

Nigeria as usually has since 1999 continued to award inflated contracts for building complex structures including roads and telecommunication networks; stadia; and electric power generating, transmitting and distribution systems. This is how Nigeria had hoped to build a reliable infrastructural network.

Nigerian roads are perpetually in a terrible condition. Every other infrastructural component is perpetually in a bad state. The refineries are perpetually waiting for the Turn Around Maintenance (TAM) to be carried out by those who built them through contracts. This is the situation after erecting four refineries beginning in the 1960s. The Egbin thermal electric power plant, the biggest in the nation, built decades ago, is perpetually waiting for a big-contract rehabilitation. The Kainji hydropower plant built by the Swedes in 1968 is again to be rehabilitated by the Swedes (see The Guardian, Nov. 13, 2003, p. 17). The situation confirms our theory that societies which merely award big contracts to foreigners to erect structures do not build-up capabilities; they perpetually suffer the stress of decaying infrastructure, indebtedness, poverty, corruption, mass unemployment and other evils. What are highly distressed nations like Nigeria and other African nations ready to do to restore hope to their people? They must set their national priorities rights, to restore hope in their societies. The Guiness Book of World Records (2004), rocorded that as of 2002, Somalia spent least on education, allocating just 0.4 per cent of its GNP to primary, secondary and tertiary education. That was followed by Nigeria (a.k.a.: the Giant of Africa), 0.7 per cent and Sierra Leone, 0.9 per cent. Also the highest budgetary expenditure on education in the world was by the New Caledonia with 13.5 per cent of its GNP. Two capitalist and industrialised nations, the U.K. and the USA spent between 5 and 6 per cent of the GNP on education, about 8 times what Nigeria spent. Nigeria's budgetary allocations to education in the period 1999-2007, respectively were: 11.3%, 8.4%, 7%, 1.8%, 7.2%, 6.8%, and 8.8%, for 1999, 2000, 2001,2002, 2003, 2004, 2005, and 2006. Compare these values with the average of 25.80% for South Africa,23.60% for Singapore and 30.0% for Ghana during the same period.

The UNDP 2003-2006 Human Development Reports ranked Nigeria 152nd among 175 nations in 2003, 151st among 175 nations in 2004, 158th among 177 nations in 2005 and 159th among 177 nations in 2006. The problem with Nigeria since 1966 has been that of a leadership without a focus and proper priority order but desirous of immediate wealth.

Quantum of Resources Needed

The economists traditionally believe that there are only two factors of production. These are labour and capital. The mainstream economist (the economic man) believe that capital is the limiting factor of production. This is why the development song of today's western intelligentsia and his student in the developing world is: Capital! Capital!! Capital!!!; Capital flows! Capital flows!! Capital flows!!! Western leaders (intelligentsia, politicians and businessmen) are wrong in assuming that there are only two factors of production. They are also wrong in claiming that capital is the limiting factor of production.

There are many resources that a nation can mobilize for industrialisation and development. Some of these are people (human resources) and material resources – money, mineral resources endowment, water, time, etc. These resources may further be grouped into the learning people – the appreciating assets (AAs) and depreciating or depletable assets (DAs). People who are not learning, mineral resources, structures and time are DAs.

To achieve industrialization, Nigeria needs to mobilize and educate about 15 (fifteen) million youths up to university level in science and engineering-related areas and also train them to acquire complementary practical skills, so that they can be equipped with the relevant production skills (RPSs). All other resources should be mobilized in support of education and training the learning people. The strategy is to develop the people, so that the people can build all the structures that mankind needs to live an enjoyable life.

Nigeria can achieve the desired objective in 20 years with proper planning. Nigeria's poorly organized universities now produces about 180,000 (one hundred and eighty thousand) graduates in a year. This needs to be increased by at least 20 per cent per year during the next 20 years to achieve the desirable objective of industrialisation.

Besides, the educational systems including primary, secondary and tertiary need to be reformed to be ready to produce the desired nation-builders. Whereas good education prepares the individual with a developed mind, knowledge and good character, the Nigerian educational system during the past 25 years has only been producing survivors – people with survivalist instincts. They are people who complete their programmes under very trying conditions. They are not nation-builders. A nation needs many millions of nation-builders to be a happy one. People with survivalist instincts do not build a nation.

Building a nation is a challenge that must be faced boldly. Nigeria has been neglecting education and training. This is the reason Nigeria has been drifting. The serious neglect of education in the period 1999 – 2007 has further aggravated the already bad situation. Every patriotic citizen should impress upon those in government that there is no alternative to giving education and training the attention they deserve. Nigeria cannot survive without developing its most important resources – the people.

Only a stupid man neglects the education and training of his children and builds houses for the illiterate and wayward children to inherit. Similarly, only a visionless national leadership neglects education and training of the youths and builds structures. It is only a visionless leadership that neglects education and training and devotes all the resources of the state to hosting various world and regional events and jamborees. The visionless leadership begs for debt forgiveness and foreign direct investment inflow and hopes that these would transform a primitive nation into an advanced one. It is only a visionless national leadership that loots a nation into indebtedness and claims that indebtedness is preventing it from funding education. Nigeria and other African nations must re-order their priorities to avoid chaos in the continent. They should moblize all necessary resources to develop the needed manpower for industrialisation.

Private Sector Contribution

There is a growing evidence that the State in the West is shifting some of the financial burden of education and job-training to the primary beneficiary, the business community. In European countries, private sector's share of the cost of training is on the increase. Table 2 shows the situation in France and Germany in the mid-1980s (Kanawaty, 1985). In both France and Germany, the private sector's share was lower in the early 1980s. The share became more than 40 per cent by the mid-1980s. It may have been increased again.

Table 2: Training Cost Sharing Formulae in France and Germany

Country	State Share (%)	Private Sector (%)	Others Share (%)	Total (%)
France	58.6	35.4	6	100.0
Germany	58.0	42.0		100.0

Source: Kanawaty (1985).

The Manufacturers Association of Nigeria (MAN) members have been protesting over the 2 per cent tax on profit in support of education(the Education Tax) in Nigeria, claiming that it is an unnecessary burden. Their reactions is expected knowing what businessmen and women are. The formal private sector in a developing nation does not plant crops; it only harvests. Foreign business organizations only come to Nigeria to make large profits. They do not get involved in long-term issues. Education and national development are long-term issues. A nation that leaves its manpower development issue to profit considerations is only working toward precipitating chaos. An educational system dependent on market forces (profit) is a useless one - one not meant to promote growth and development. However, business organisation in Europe and America make compulsory and voluntary contributions to funding education and research. They should do the same in Nigeria.

Apart from the issue of cost sharing, governments in progressive nations are tying to make their training systems as a whole work as efficiently as possible. Technologically advanced countries are trying to improve their training policies, training legislation and support for various training activities and institutions through national or international initiatives, to establish coordinating mechanisms. Developing nations ought to do more.

Efforts in Nigeria should now go beyond arbitrary contributions like 2% profit-tax, to contributing a known percentage of education and training cost as it is done in Europe. Let it be known that the OPS (Organized Private Sector) contributes 20 per cent or so, of the total cost of education and training in Nigeria. This approach would be more meaningful and comparable.

Savings From Reduced Import Pressure

One of Nigeria's 'draining pipes' over the decades has been importation. The so-called OPS is a parasitic fluke that exists to use the foreign exchange that it cannot earn, to import goods indiscriminately. In the mid-1980s, it was estimated that foreign exchange leakage (unnecessary expenditure) was more than N2 billion naira (at the time one naira exchange for about two United States dollars) (Adedeji,

124

1985). Today, the ordinary Nigerian is experiencing serious economic stress because the Nigerian political leaders and their private sector friends have looted Nigeria into punury. It is those who have stashed over $170 billion (one hundred and seventy billion dollars) away in foreign accounts that have been clamouring for the economy to be sold to them and have now bought public assets at give-a-way prices. This cannot produce the relevant knowledge and skills for producing the things Nigeria imports blindly today. There is no alternative to acquiring the knowledge and skills that would enable Nigeria to achieve industrialisation. This is what government and the investing public, learning and educational institutions and those who produce goods and provide services must cooperate to achieve speedily in all developing nations, including Nigeria.

The SSS-2-U-4 practical skills-acquiring scheme will readily build-up the knowledge-and-skills framework that would enable Nigeria to achieve industrialisation. The real growth that would be initiated by the proposed framework would reduce importation pressure. The reduction in importation expenditure should be used to support the new scheme. Other African nations can adopt similar schemes and expect measurable benefits in a short time.

10

LESSONS OF HISTORY

European Experience:

History shows that Britain and France spent about 2000 years before achieving modern industrialization (Carrington and Jackson, 1954). But the positive changes which characterized the later stages of their evolutionary development voyage are worth noting.

During the fourteenth and fifteenth centuries, the design of apparatus and precision instruments in Europe were usually done by craftsmen working empirically and with little theoretical knowledge; the occasional experimentalist in the ranks of theoretical science was likely to work alone, too, in private laboratories without employing the services of craftsmen. In the slow growth period therefore, there was no cooperation between the theoretician and the artisan/craftsman in Europe (Gottschalk, *et al.*, 1969). But this situation changed in the sixteenth and seventeenth centuries; the theoretician and the craftsman began to work together. It brought many benefits to Europeans, especially the English. For example, it was at that time that in the mines of Erzgebirge (craftsman) that Agricola (theorist) laid the foundation for his treatise on metallurgy and it was in a Viena arsenal that Galileo made his famous contributions to the science of machines and astronomy (Gottschalk, *et al.*, 1969). It was probably this late cooperation in British development history that set the stage for the world's first Industrial Revolution. The cooperation period has also been described as the Mechanical Period (Lilley, 1965; and Forbes, 1958). It was during the cooperation period that mechanical treatise were prepared and the basis for the factory system established. It was probably the conscious blending of theoretical and practical skills which prepared Britain for the experience which no other society had had. Britain did not emphasize the build-up of complex infrastructure before achieving the desirable feat.

By 1750, there were only 12 private banks in England. The number had risen to 843 in 1821 with 62 located in London. The large increase in the number of private banks was the result of the industrial revolution (1760-1850); the Bank of England had been founded in 1694 for the purpose of lending money to the Government (Hanson, 1977). Private banking was often at first only a sideline to a manufacturer's or a merchant's main business. For example, the Lloyd's Bank was established by Samuel Lloyd who was in iron and steel business in Birmingham. The growth of the banking industry thus was post-industrial in England; industrialization produces a viable banking system. France, Germany, Sweden and other European nations had similar experiences.

Asian Experience

The Japanese claim that the existence of their nation dates back to about 600 B.C., although more objective sources suggest 300 B.C. (Reischaur, 1970). When Commodore Matthew Perry of the United States navy entered the Edo Bay in Japan in 1854, about 2154 years after the existence of the nation, on board the steam frigate, Susquehanna, most Japanese apparently had not seen such a vessel, much less a whole flotilla (*Time Magazine*, 1983). Japan had been an isolated society. Americans actually forced their way into Japan, to open it up to the outside world. This humiliation led to the subtle *coup d'etat*, popularly known as the "Meiji Restoration" in 1868.

Prior to the Restoration, education in Japan had been restricted to a narrow scope, only a certain class enjoyed its benefits and indeed loyalty to family and hereditary rights took precedence over education. The subjects of study were also limited to Chinese literature with emphasis on morals. Soon after the Restoration, the Meiji Government directed serious changes in the subjects studied.

The Government did not waste time establishing model industries which encouraged Japanese to build factories modeled after those established by the Government. Japanese Government sent experts to provinces to present lectures and practical experimentation and demonstration. The Government also sent student-manufacturers and merchants abroad to investigate the conditions of manufacture and trade. By so doing, the Government was making conscious efforts to blend theoretical and practical skills. These efforts quickly built up the skill-framework needed to support high productivity.

The Restoration met Japan an agrarian nation. There were few, if any industries of importance in Japan at that time (Stead, 1906). The conscious effort toward education, development of and blending of theory and practice, rapidly transformed agrarian Japan into an industrialized nation. The real start of Japan's modern economic growth can be placed in the 20 years period 1886-1905. In the early 1880's, raw silk, tea and rice (primary commodities) accounted for over two-thirds of Japan's export. But by 1905, more than half of Japanese exports was machine-made goods, consisting of cotton yarns and cotton, and silk-piece goods (Hall, 1971). Modern economic transformation for Japan took place during the period 300 B.C. – 1905, some 2200 years, but the 20-year activities during the period 1886-1905 are worth noting.

China has one of the earliest recorded history in the world, and it is known as one of the great medieval civilizations. Chinese, Indian, and Islamic cultures were the great medieval civilizations (Gottschalk, *et al.*, 1969). The Chinese claim that their history began about 4000 B.C., but research suggests that there was indeed an advanced civilization in the area occupied by China today as early as 1000 B.C., although there were separate local cultures each developing on its own around 2500 B.C. in the same region (Eberhard, 1950).

China was ruled by dynasties for a long time. A dynasty is a line of kings. There was already 28 principal dynasties in North and South China by 618 A.D. It was all political struggle for power; the Chinese were either fighting a civil war, or fighting against external aggression. That was the situation till 1911. The last king had died in 1908 but a strong lady held on till 1911 when she was overthrown. China therefore became a Republic in 1911 (Stokes and Stokes, 1975).

The tussle over power and external aggression continued after China became a Republic. The Chinese were under foreign domination for years. Indeed, it was

World War II that removed China from the clutches of the pugnacious Japanese. After the Japanese withdrew from China, the Nationalist and the Chinese Communist Party (CCP) led by Mao Zegung had to fight it out. The CCP won and it together with other minor democratic parties formed the People's Republic of China (PRC) in 1949, and the Nationalist withdrew to Taiwan. This is the origin of China and Taiwan as separated brothers.

In 1949, the Chinese economy was in chaos. The Russians on whom they had depended for a long time had quarreled with them and they had stripped Manchuria, the most built-up city of everything. The transport system was in ruins, and the currency was worthless.

The Chinese used the resource they have in abundance, people. "Let the people walk on two legs" said Mao Zegung, "Let the native skills and local materials supplement modern technology" (Stokes and Stokes, 1975). Mao probably meant to link learning efforts in educational institutions with traditional skills of artisans/craftsmen. Everyone in the Chinese communes worked together. The Great Leap, 1958-1961 was also based on the principle of the educated and traditional people working together. This is how the Chinese having crawled during the period 2500 B.C. – 1949, about 4449 years, accelerated modernization to become the fastest growing economy in the world today.

CONCERTED EFFORTS NEEDED

All governments need help. Governments are built by many people; no single great leader alone builds a good government. The quality of any government again depends much more on the sum of the small leadership qualities in many of its citizens than on the leadership quality of one great leader. Let us help our government and ourselves.

You have read our proposals. If you have any doubt about any of the proposals, try to reach us so that we can discuss it. But if you agree with us that we have found how to promote rapid industrilisation and solve mass unemployment problem, help to spread the good news fast. Tell your neighbour of our findings. Write to tell government officials that we have found solution to mass unemployment problem. This is how government can adopt the proposal speedily and stimulate sustainable economic growth and accelerated industrialization in Nigeria and other African nations. Let us help our governments and ourselves.

REFERENCES

Abubakar, Atiku (1999). 'Nigeria: Dawn of a new day,' an address presented as Vice-President of Nigeria in the Seminar organized by the World Bank and IMF in Washington, D.C., U.S.A., Sept. 26. See also *The Guardian*, Monday Oct. 4, 1999, p. 19.

Adedeji, A. (1993). Africa and Orthodox Structural Adjustment Programmes: Perception, Policy and Politics, a paper presented during the United Nations University (UNU) Symposium on the Challenges of African Development: Structural Adjustment Policies and Implementation, UNU Headquarters, Tokyo, Oct. 1.

Adedeji, A. (1985). Lessons of experience, in *West Africa Weekly Magazine, August*.

African Development Bank (1997). *African Development Bank Report* 1997, Oxford University Press, New York.

Aluko, S.A.; O.A. Oguntoye and Y.A.O. Afonja (1973). Small-Scale Industries: Mid-Western State, Kwara State and Lagos State, Industrial Research Unit (IRU), Department of Economics, University of Ife (Obafemi Awolowo University), Ile-Ife, Nigeria.

Aluko, S.A.; O.A. Oguntoye and Y.A.O. Afonja (1972). Small-Scale Industries: Western State of Nigeria, The IRU, Dept. of Economics, University of Ife, Ile-Ife, Nigeria.

Amrine, H., T. Ritchey and O.S.H. Hulley (1982). *Manufacturing Organisation and Management*, Fourth Edition, Prentice-Hall, Inc., Englewood Cliff, New Jersey, U.S.A.

Ani, A. (1996-97). Texts of Federal Budget Breakdown, Ministry of Finance, Abuja.

Ani, A. (1995). Economic Decline, check private sector's Antics, *Vanguard*, Dec. 22, p. 15.

Arikawe, Akin (2002). Nigeria Services Debts with $7.17 billion in three years, a presentation in a public forum (see *The Guardian*, Monday, Dec. 30, 2002, p. 19).

Arikawe, Akin (2003). Nigeria's loans, 40 per cent lost in transit, a presentation in public forum (see *The Guardian*, Sunday, Oct. 12, 2003, p. A30.

Baldwin, L.D. (1969). *The Stream of American History,* Fourth Edition, Van Nostrant Reinhold Co., New York.

Bartlett, I., E. Fenton, D. Fowler and S. Mandelbaum (1969). *A New History of the United States, An Inquiry Approach, Holt Social Studies Curriculum,* Edwin Fenton (General Editor), Holt, Rinechart and Winston, Inc., U.S.A.

Barros, R.L.P., M. de Fatima, F. de Praiva and C.L.S. Sisinno (2003). Cleaner Production Challenges in B razilian SMEs, UNEP *Industry and Environment,* Vol. 26, No.4, October-December, p. 26-28.

Baseline Economic Survey of Small and Medium Scale Industries in Nigeria (2004), Prepared by NISER, Ibadan, Nigeria, for the CBN, Abuja, Nigeria.

Becker, D.E. (1983). *Managing Production Systems,* Green Edition, Printed in the United States.

Bello, U.K. (1987). Fiscal Policy Implementation of Structural Adjustment Programme (SAP), a paper presented at the First Biennial Conference of the Faculty of Business Administration, University of Lagos, Lagos, Nigeria, Oct. 26-28.

Brautsaset, K. (1990). Engineering Education in Norway and Reflections on Engineering Education in General, *Proceedings of the 1990 Annual Conference of the American Society of Engineering Education* (ASEE) in Toronto, Canada, pp. 406-410.

Bright, P. and C. van Lamsweerde (1993). Environmental Education and Training in the Royal Dutch/Shell Group of Companies, *United Nations Environmental Programme (UNEP) Industry and Environment*, October – December, pp. 28-32.

Bulletin of Science and Technology & Society. Vol. 4, pp. 519-525, 1984.

Cagan, P. (1956). The Monetary Dynamics of Hyper-inflation in M. Friedman (ed.), Studies in *The Quantity Theory of Money*, Chicago University Press, Chicago, U.S.A.

Cardwell, D.S.L. (1974). *Turning-Points in Western Technology: A study of Technology, Science and History*, Science History Publication, New York.

Carrington, C.E. and J.H. Jackson (1954). *A History of England*, Cambridge University Press, England.

Chinese Statistical Bureau (1996), Beijin, China.

Cobb, C. and P. Douglas (1928). A Theory of Production, *American Economic Review Supplement*, March.

Collier, P. (2003). A presentation in the Leon Sullivan Summit in Abuja, Nigeria, July (see also *The Guardian*, Monday, December 22, 2003, P. 17).

Collier, P. (2003a). Critical success factors in implementing a country's growth strategy, a paper presented in the Tenth Nigerian Economic Summit with the them: Nigeria: Partering for Growth and Transformation, in Abuja, Nigeria, Sept. 10-12.

Daily Times, Nigerian Edition, Monday, April 15, 1991, p. 25.

Daley, W. (1998). Keynote Address at the International Herald Tribune 2-day South African .Trade and Investment Summit in Cape Town. South Africa, Dec. 1-2.

Davies, R.T. (1969). *Documents Illustrating the History of Civilization in Medieval England 1066-1500*, Methuen & Co. Ltd., London.

Domar, E.D. (1946). Capital Expansion, Rate of Growth and Development, *Econometrica* 14, pp. 137-147.

Drucker, P.E. (1954). *The Practice of Management*, Harper and Row Publishers, New York.

Eberhard, W. (1950). *A History of China*, Routledge and Kegan Paul, London.

Egwaikhide, F.O. (1997). Import Substitution Industrialization in Nigeria: A selective Review, *Nigerian J. Economic and Social Studies (NJESS)*, Vol. 39, No. 2, pp. 183-203.

El-Rufai, N. (2007). How Nigeria can be among 20 largest economies in the world, a Keynote address presented in March, 2007 at Abuja. See also, VANGUARD, Wednesday, March 27, 2007, p.13.

Ernle, R.E.P (1822). English Farming Past and Present, London, cited in *Agriculture and Structural Transformation*, Third Printing, 1979, Oxford University Press, New York, B.F. Johnson and P.Kilb (authors).

Fagg, J.E. (1969). *Latin America: A General History*, 2nd Edition,

The Macmillan Co., Collier-Macmillan Ltd., London.

Federal Government of Nigeria (1962). *First National Plan 1962-68*, Ministry of Finance, Lagos.

Forbes, R.J. (1958). *Man the Maker: A History of Technology and Engineering*. Constable and Co. Ltd., New York.

Galbraith, J.K. (1967). *The New Industrial State*, Houghton Mifflin Company, Boston, U.S.A.

Gerschenkron, A. (1966). *Economic Backwardness in Historical Perspective: A Book of Essays*, Harvard University Press, Cambridge, U.S.A.

Girvan, N.P. (1983). *Technology policies for small developing economies, A study of the Caribbean, Caribbean Technology Policy studies Project*, Copyrighted by the Institute of Social and Economic Research of the West Indies, Mona, Jamaica.

Glahe, F.R. (1977). *Macroeconomics Theory and Policy*, Second Edition, Harcourt Brace Jovanovich, Inc., New York.

Gottschalk, L., L.G. Mackinney and E.H. Pritchard (1969). *The Foundation of the Modern World, Inter. Commission for a History of Mankind, Culture and Scientific Development*, Vol. II, Harper and Row, New York.

Hall, J.W. (1971). *Japan: from Historic to Modern Times*, Second Print, Delacorte Press, New York.

Hanson, J.L. (1977). *A Textbook of Economics*. Seventh Edition (Low Price Series). The English Language Book Society and Mc Donald and Evans Ltd., London.

Harrod, R.F. (1939). An Essay in dynamic theory, *Economic Journal*, Vol. 49, pp. 14-33.

Hoogvelt, A.M.M. (1976). *The Sociology of Developing Societies*, The Macmillan Press, Bungay, England.

Ilori, B. (1998). Institutional Framework for Plan and Budget Monitoring and Evaluation, a paper presented in the Workshop on Plan and Budget Monitoring and Evaluation, organized by the National Center for Economic Management and Administration (NCEMA), Ibadan, March 2-9.

Inman, J.E. (1984). *The Regulatory Environment of Business*, John Wiley & Sons., New York.

International Business Week (1988). Human capital: The Decline of America's workforce, Sept. 19, A McGraw-Hill Publication, U.S.A.

International Institute of Strategic Studies (2001). Military balance 2001/2002 Report (see also *The Guardian*, Thursday, Nov. 1, 2001, p. 3).

International Labour Organisation (1991). *Gains of Self-employment*, ILO Bulletin, Geneva.

ILO (1998). *Global Employment Trends: The Outlook is Grim*, ILO, Geneva.

ILO (2006). *ILO Global Economic Report*, ILO, Switzerland.

Johnstone, O.B. (1985). *Sharing the Cost of Higher Education*, College Board Publications, New York.

Jones, E.L. (1967). *Agricultrue and Economic Growth in England* 1650-1815, london.

Kanawaty, G. (1985). Training for a changing World: Some general reflections, *Int. Labour Review,* Vol. 124, No. 54, July – Aug., 401-409.

Klausmeier, H.J. (1985). *Educational Psychology,* Fifth Edition, Harper and Row, New York.

Keynes, J.M. (1936). *The General Theory of Employment, Interest and Money,* Harcourt Brace and World, New York.

Lawal, H. (2006). Self-employment, Best Option for Youths Says Minister, in *The Guardian,* Thursday, September 23rd, 2004, p.6.

Lee, D. (1852). Annual Report New York State Agricultural Society (1886), p. 158, cited in C.H. Danholf (1969): *Changes in Agriculture: the Northern United States,* 1820-1870, Harvard University Press, Cambridge, U.S.A.

Lewis, W.A. (1972). *Theory of Economic Growth.* Tenth Printing, Unwin University Book, London.

Lilley, W.A. (1965). *Men, Machines and History: The story of tools and machines in relation to social progress,* Lawrence Wishart, New York.

Lodge, G.C. (1977). *Managerial Implications of ideological change, The Ethics of Corporate Conduct,* Prentice-Hall, Inc., Englewood Cliff, New Jersey.

Lodge, G.C. (1977a). Ibid.

Manufacturers' Association of Nigeria (MAN) (1995). *1995 Report,* MAN's House, Lagos.

MAN (1987). *Nigeria: Industrial Directory,* MAN's House, Lagos.

Marglin, S.A.: (1991). Lesson of the Golden Age: An Overview, in *The Golden Age of capitalism, Reinterpreting the Post-War Experience*, edited by Stephen Marglin and Juliet Schor, Clarendon Press, Oxford, England.

Marx, K. (1867). *Capital*, International Publishers, New York, 1967.

Mondadori, A. (editor) (1985). *100 Years of the Automobile*, W.H. Smith Publishers, New York.

Moore, T. (1801). The Great Error in American Agriculture Exposed. Baltimore, U.S.A., cited in: C.H. Danhof (1969): *Changes in Agriculture: The Northern United States*, 1820-1870, Harvard University Press, Cambridge.

Naiyeju, Kayode (2003). Performance of the Nigerian 2003 budget, a presentation in a budget interactive session with the House of Representative, Abuja. Also see *The Guardian*, Wednesday, October 1, 2003, backpage.

National Universities Commission (1995). Nigerian University System. A parastatals Past, Present and Future, A Report prepared for the National Constitution Conference Committee on Civil Service and Parastatals, Abuja.

Ndiokho, B.U. (1998). Woes of Economy by Ndiokho: in *The Guardian*, Monday, May 18, frontpage.

Nigeiran Tribune, Thursday, July 6, 2006 frontpage (Britain takes away N6.8 trillion from Africa in one year).

Obasanjo, O. (2005). We Must Set Our Hearts for the Best, an Address Presented to the National Assembly, on the National Reform Conference and Recent Debts Relief Granted Nigeria by President Obasanjo, July 26th, 2005, Abuja.

Obibiaku, O. (2005). 'Agricultural Entrepreneurship Development: Roadmap to Nigeria's Economic Diversification,' British Department for International Development (DFID), Nigeria.

Observatory of European SMEs (2001), Cited by UNEP Industry and Environment, Vol. 26, No. 4, October-December, 2003, p.4.

Ohiwerei, F. (1998). Why Nigeria Must Liberalise by Ohiwerei, *The Guardian*, February 9, p. 37.

Ogbimi, F.E. (1988). Technological Development: Human Resource and Self-reliance, *Proceedings of the 1988 Annual Conference of the Nigerian Society of Engineers (NSE)*, Abeokuta, pp. 52-61.

Ogbimi, F.E. (1990). The Nature of Technological Development: Implications for Engineering Education and Technology Transfer, a paper presented during the 1990 ASEE Annual Conference in Toronto, Canada.

Ogbimi, F.E. (1990a). Managing Education-Production Linkages for Rapid Economic Growth in Developing Nations, *Proceedings of the 1990 Annual Conference of the Nigerian Society of Engineers (NSE)*, pp. 106-111.

Ogbimi, F.E. (1990b). Establishing a Policy Framework for Rapid Technological Advancement in Nigeria, *The Nigerian Engineer,* Vol. No. 25, No. 3, p.1-8.

Ogbimi, F.E. (1991). Managing Education-Production Linkages: Bridging the Gap between Theoretical and Practical Skills in Nigeria, *Proceedings of the Conference jointly organized by Council for Registered Engineers of Nigeria (COREN) and Committee of Deans of Engineering and Technological Institutions* (CODET) in Lagos, July 16-19, pp. 22-32.

Ogbimi, F.E. (1991a). Innovative Maintenance as a Pre-requisite for Industrialization in Third World Nations, *Proceedings of the 1991 Annual Conference of the Nigerian Society of Engineers (NSE)*, pp. 114-120.

Ogbimi, F.E. (1992). Continuing Engineering Education: Essential Linkage Programme for Rapid Technological Growth in Nigeria, *Proceedings of the 5th World Conference of The International Association of Continuing Engineering Education (IACEE)*, Espoo, Finland, June 2-5.

Ogbimi, F.E. (1992a). Improving Productivity in the African Production System: The Nigerian Small and Medium Scale Enterprise, *Proceedings of the 1992 NSE Annual Conference*, pp.114-127.

Ogbimi, F.E. (1994). Understanding the Problem of Sourcing Raw Materials in Third World Nations: The Nigerian Case, Unpublished.

Ogbimi, F.E. (1994a). Distortions in Economy: Causes, Measurement and Management, Unpublished.

Ogbimi, F.,E. (1994b). Initiating a Rapid Capability-Building Agricultural Mechanization Programme in Nigeria (A Refereed Monograph).

Ogbimi, F.,E. (1995). A Critique of Nigerian Technology Acquisition Experience 1960-95: Initiating Rapid Development (Refereed Monograph).

Ogbimi, F.E. (1995a). Solution to Co-Existent Low Productivity, High Unemployment and High Inflation, *Nigerian J. Economic and Social Studies (NJESS)*, Vol. 37, No. 3, pp. 223-251.

Ogbimi, F.E. (1996). Origin and Impact of International Technology Transfer as a Development Strategy, Unpublished.

Ogbimi, F.E. (1996a). Understanding the Primary Source of Sustainable Economic Growth, a Monograph.

Ogbimi, F.E. (1997). 6-3-3-4-4 Educational System: Framework for Developing Engineers for Rapid Industrialization in Nigeria, *Proceedings of the 1997 Annual Conference of the NSE*, pp. 141-150.

Ogbimi, F.E. (1997a). Causes and Remedies for Poverty in Nigeria, a Monograph.

Ogbimi, F.E. (1998). SSS-2-U-4 Practical Skills-Acquisition Framework: Instrument for Appropriate university Enrolment, Eliminating Unemployment and Programmed Industrialization in Nigeria, in, *Bridging Tertiary Institutions and Labour Market in Nigeria*, Ebebe Ukpong, editor, National Manpower Board.

Ogbimi, F.E. (1998a). Introducing growth elements into Nigeria's planning process, a Monograph.

Ogbimi, F.E. (1999). The Concept of Technological Framework and Its Relevance in Planing for Developing Nations, *Proceedings of the 1999 Annual Conference of the Nigerian Society of Engineers (NSE)* in Ilorin, Nigeria, pp. 228-245.

Ogbimi, F.E. (2006). *Understanding Why Education and Training are Indispensable to Rapid Industrialisation and Development,* Society for Linking Education and Problems Publication, Obafemi Awolowo University, Ile-Ife, Nigeria.

Ogbimi, F.E. and S. Adjebeng-Asem, (1994). Improving Performance in the S&T Policy Process in Nigeria, *N.S.E. Technical Transactions*, Vol. 29, No. 3, July-Sept., pp. 30-39.

Ogbimi, F.E. and J.B. Akarakiri (1997). Developing the Pulp and Paper industry in Nigeria, A Research Report Prepared for NISER,

Ibadan, by Technology Planning and Development Unit (TPDU), Obafemi Awolowo University, Ile-Ife, Nigeria.

Okigbo, P.N.C.(1989). *National Development Planning in Nigeria 1900-92*, Fourth Dimension Publishing Co. Ltd., Enugu.

Okonjo-Iweala, N. (2005). Building a World Free of Graft, in *The Guardian*, Tuesday, April 5, p.21.

Onimode, B. (1982*). Imperialism and underdevelopment in Nigeria*, Macmillan Press, London.

Ormerod, P. (1994). *The Death of Economics*, Faber and Faber, London.

Phillips, A.W. (1958). The relation between unemployment and the rate of change of money wage rates in the United Kingdom 1861-1957, *Economica*, 25 (November): 283-299.

Popoola, S.O. (1998). Qualitative Information Based Monitoring and Evaluation Conditions and Benefits, a paper presented in the Workshop on Plan and Budget Monitoring and Evaluation, Organized by NCEMA, Ibadan, March 2-9.

Quarcoo, P.K. (1990). Structural Adjustment Programme in Sub-Saharan Africa: Evolution of Approaches, *African Development*, Vol. 2, No. 2, pp. 1-7.

Reischaur, E.O. (1970). *Japan: the Story of a Nation*, Buckworth, London.

Rostow, W.W. (1960). *The Stages of Economic Growth: A Non-Communist Manifesto*, Cambridge University Press, England.

Rostow, W.W. (1980). *Why Poor Nations get Richer and the Rich Slow Down: Essay in the Marshallian Long Period*, University of Texas Press, Austin, Texas, U.S.A.

Russell, B. (1967). *History of Western Philosophy*, George Allen and Unwin Ltd., London.

Schumpeter, J.A. (1934). *The Theory of Economic Development*, Oxford University Press.

Smith, Adam (1776). *An Inquiry into the Nature and Causes of the Wealth of Nations* (2 Vols.) Printed for W. Strahan and T. Cadwell in The Strand, London.

Stahl, J.P. (1990). A New Universal Learning Curve, *Proceedings of the 1990 Annual Conference of the ASEE* in Canada, pp. 1863-68.

Stead, A. (1906). *Great Japan: A Study in National Efficiency*, John Lane the Bodley Head, London.

Stokes, J. and G. Stokes (1975). *The People's Republic of China*, Ernest Ben, Ltd., London.

Stolper, G., K. Hauser and K. Barchard (1967). *Germany 1870-1940, Translated by Toni Stolper*, Weidfeld and Nicolson, London.

The Guardian, Nigerian Edition, Wed. Feb. 25, 1998, p. 40.

The Guardian, Nigerian Edition, May 29, 1998, p. 5.

The Guardian, Thursday, Oct. 7, 1999, p. 17.

The Guardian, Thursday, Nov. 13, 2003, p. 17 (Nigeria, Sweden discuss Kainji power station's rehabilitation plan).

Time Magazine (1983). Japan: A Nation in Search of Itself, Special Issue, Aug. 1, p. 18.

Trevelyan, G.M. (1948). *History of England*, Longmans Green Co., London.

Turner, G. (1963). *The Carmaker,* Eyre and Spottis-Woode, London.

Uga, E. (1998). Overview of development Planning Experience in Nigeria, a paper presented in the workshop on Plan and Budget Monitoring and Evaluation, organized by NCEMA, Ibadan, March 2-9.

UNDP (1990-2006). *Human Development Reports*, Oxford University Press, Oxford.

UNEP Industry and Environment (2003). Big Challenge for Small Business: Sustainability and SMEs, Vol. 26, No. 4, October-December, p. 4.

U.S. Census Bureau (2000).*2000 Census,* Washington, D.C., USA.

UNIDO (1988). *Nigeria: Industrial Restructuring through Policy Reform*, Industrial Development Review Series, prepared by the Regional and Country Studies Branch, PPD 100, 21, p. xiii.

UNIDO (1989). *New Technologies and Global Industrialisation Prospects for Developing Countries,* PPD 141, Nov. 1989.S

Vaitos, C. (1975). The process of commercialization of technology in the Andeen pact, in H. Radice (ed.) *International Firms and Modern Imperialism,* Penguim Press, London, p. 183.

Vision 2010 Committee (1997). *Report of the Vision 2010 Committee*: Main Report, Sept., the Presidency, Abuja.

Wiet, G., V. Elisseeff, P. Wolff and J. Naudon (1975). *The Great Medieval Civilization translated from the French, International Commission for a History of Mankind, Culture and Scientific Development*, Vol. III, Harper and Row, New York, p. 468.

World Bank (2006). Poverty: Africa is a tragedy-World Bank, in *The Punch, Nigeria,* Saturday, September 16th, 2006, p.8.

World Bank and IMF (2006). Africa to Get 2.1% of World Economy - IMF, World Bank, in *Daily Independent,* Monday, August 7, 2006, frontpage (A1).

Some other titles in the series

* Understanding Why Capital Investment Cannot Promote Sustainable Economic Growth and Industrialisation.

* Understanding Why Learning is the Primary Source of Sustainable Economic Growth, Industrialisation and Development.

* Causes and Remedies for Poverty in Africa.

* Understanding Why Education and Training are Indispensable to Rapid Industrialisation and Development.

* Understanding the Theory and Practice of Federalism and Democracy.

* Why Privatisation is Promoting Unemployment and Poverty and Delaying Industrialisation in Africa.

Send inquiries about any of these titles to:

> Prof. F. E. Ogbimi,
> Coordinator, SOLEP,
> P. O. Box 1940,
> O. A.U. Post Office,
> Obafemi Awolowo University,
> Ile-Ife, Nigeria
> OR (ogbimi@solep.org)